MONEY SKILLS FOR KIDS

A Beginner's Guide to Earning, Saving, and Spending Wisely.

Everything Tweens Should Know About Personal Finance.

FERNE BOWE

Money Skills for Kids. A Beginner's Guide to Earning, Saving, and Spending Wisely. Everything Tweens Should Know About Personal Finance.

Published by: Bemberton Ltd

ISBN: 978-1-915833-20-4

Disclaimer: The information in this book is general and designed to be for information only. While every effort has been made to ensure it is wholly accurate and complete, it is for general information only. It is not intended, nor should it be taken, as professional advice. The author gives no warranties or undertakings whatsoever concerning the content. The reader should consult a professional financial advisor before making significant decisions regarding finances or money matters. The reader accepts that the author is not responsible for any action, including but not limited to losses, both directly or indirectly incurred by the reader as a result of the content in this book.

Get your **FREE** printable copy of the
"Life Skills for Tweens Workbook"

WITH OVER 80 FUN ACTIVITIES JUST FOR TWEENS!

Scan the code to download your FREE printable copy

TABLE OF CONTENTS

INTRODUCTION

Welcome to *Money Skills for Kids.*

Have you ever stared longingly at the newest video game or the latest gadget, wishing you had a bit more money to buy it? Maybe you saved up your allowance, only to realize you're a few dollars short; or perhaps you've thought about earning more, but you're not sure how to start. If any of this sounds familiar, don't worry—you're not alone.

Understanding money and how it works can sometimes feel like trying to decode a secret language. That's where this book comes in.

In a world where a handful of coins, a few pieces of paper, and some digital numbers on a screen can transform into books, toys, and even family vacations, understanding money is like having a superpower. This book is your personal guide to start developing this power!

This book will take you on a fascinating journey to discover what money really is and how you can earn it, save it, and even spend it (wisely, of course!). But we won't stop there. We'll explore how you can grow your money, learn the art of budgeting, and keep your money safe and secure.

Each chapter is filled with interesting facts, a hands-on activity, and real-life examples to make learning about money engaging and fun. By the time you reach the end of this book, you'll have uncovered the secret to making smart money choices. These skills will serve you well now and when you're grown up.

Here's a sneak peek at some of the information we'll cover:

- The fascinating world of money and how it works
- The art of budgeting and saving like a pro
- The important difference between needs and wants
- A beginner's guide to growing your money through investing
- How to keep your money safe and secure

While the following chapters are written for kids, we encourage parents to join us in this learning journey. Their participation will help ensure the lessons we cover move from the pages of this book into your everyday life. This way, you're not just learning about money in theory, but also becoming a confident money manager in practice.

We hope you and your parents will find *Money Skills for Kids* to be a valuable tool and a rewarding educational adventure.

Are you ready? Let's embark on this exciting journey together!

Please note: This book's information is general and designed to be for information only. While every effort has been made to ensure it is accurate, it is for general educational purposes only and is not intended, nor should it be taken, as professional financial advice. It is essential to consult with a qualified financial advisor before making any financial decisions. The author and publisher are not responsible for any actions taken based on the information presented in this book.

CHAPTER 1:

UNDERSTANDING MONEY

WHAT IS MONEY?

Have you ever wondered what money truly is? Well, it's more than just the coins you can feel in your pocket or the colorful notes stashed in your wallet. At its core, money is a tool that holds a particular value, kind of like a key that can unlock numerous goods and services for you.

Money is your ticket to trade. It allows you to exchange what you have—your money—for the things you want or need. That's why money is often called a "medium of exchange." Think of it like swapping. You give a certain amount of money, and in return, you receive a product or service. It's like the universal language of trade that everyone understands.

For example, say you want to buy a shiny new bike for $250. To make that bike yours, you have to hand over $250, and in return, you get the bike. Simple.

The money we use is issued by the government and comes in different shapes and sizes—coins and banknotes—each symbolizing a different value that everyone acknowledges and accepts.

When people talk about money, they often use the term "currency." This refers to the physical forms of money, such as coins and banknotes, specific to a particular country.

Every country has its own unique currency. For example, in the United States, they use the dollar. If you go to Japan, you'll need yen. In the United Kingdom, they use pounds. If you're visiting India, you'll be spending rupees. And in Mexico, you'll come across pesos. These are all different types of currency, each used within their own countries. Money might look different in every country, but it all serves the same purpose—it's a key to trade.

DID YOU KNOW? *Dollar bills are not made of ordinary paper. They are made of a special paper called "currency paper," composed of 75% cotton and 25% linen fibers. This combination makes them more durable and helps them withstand the wear and tear of everyday use. Still, the average life of a one-dollar bill is only 18 months.*

HISTORY OF MONEY

Imagine you want a new video game, but instead of going to the store to buy it, you have to find someone willing to trade the video game for something you already own. Maybe they want your skateboard, and you could agree to swap it for the video game. Sounds pretty complicated, doesn't it? Well, that's what people did before money existed. They used trading (or "bartering") to get the things they needed.

Now, let's say it is a long time ago and you have a cow, but what you really want is a horse. In this case, because there was no money, you would have had to find someone who had a horse but who wanted a cow, and who was willing to agree to the exchange. They would have to agree that it was a fair trade, and you'd have to walk your cow to the person's farm to make the trade.

As you can see, bartering was not an easy thing to do. It was not always possible to find someone willing to make a trade, people had to carry their goods long distances, and it was not always easy to agree on the value of the items they were trading to make sure the trade was fair and of equal value.

That's why physical money was created. Money solved the issues involved in trading because the value was recognized and agreed upon by everyone to ensure that the exchange was equal. Plus, money was easier to carry around than a cow or a horse.

> ***DID YOU KNOW?*** *Money dates back thousands of years. The earliest coins were made of precious metals like silver and gold, but the first use of paper money was in ancient China around the 7th century.*

The next time you go out to the store to buy a loaf of bread, just be glad you can use the coins or notes in your pocket instead of carrying a cow!

DIFFERENT FORMS OF MONEY

When you think of money, you probably think of cash. If so, you're right—cash is a form of money! But there are other forms of money, as well.

Here are some of the different forms of money:

Cash

Cash is the simplest form of money, consisting of coins and paper money.

Checks

Checks are numbered pieces of paper issued by banks saying it's ok to pay someone by having the money deducted from your bank account. Other forms of money have become more popular, and checks aren't used as much today.

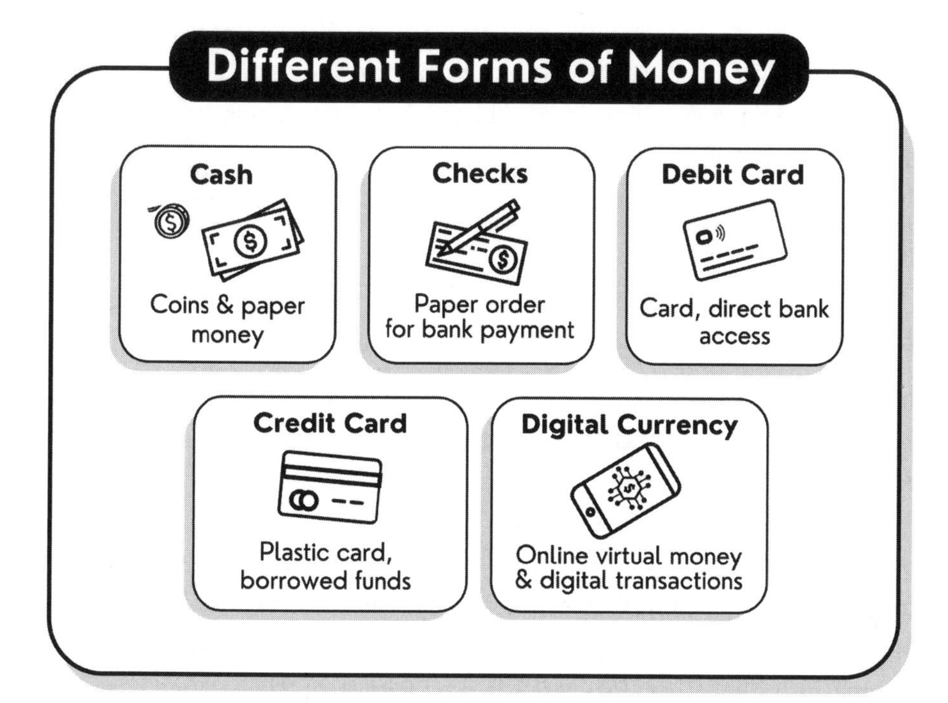

Debit Cards

A debit card is a special card that works like a combination of a check and cash. It's issued by a bank and used to buy things, just like you would with cash. But instead of carrying around cash, you can use a debit card to pay for things.

When you use a debit card, the money for your purchase is taken straight from your bank account. Banks usually don't give debit cards to kids, as you need an adult account. However, there are a number of accounts designed for kids and their parents that offer prepaid debit cards.

Prepaid debit cards for kids are usually managed by parents through an app. This means parents can put money on the card, control how it is used, and have visibility on purchases. Some apps also have features that allow parents to assign pocket money when chores are completed. This is a great way to help kids learn about money management and spending responsibly.

Credit Cards

A credit card is issued by a bank and can be used to make purchases. It works a bit differently than a debit card. When you use a credit card, you buy things now but pay for them later.

Every month, you'll get a bill from the bank for the things you bought on your credit card. It's essential to pay this bill on time. If you don't pay the total amount every month, the bank will charge you extra money, called interest. Interest is a percentage of the balance that you still owe. This means you have to pay more money back to the bank.

The bank decides how much money you can spend with the credit card. The bank is lending you this money to make purchases, and you must pay it back. If you can't pay it back in one month, the bank charges you interest on the remaining balance. As with debit cards, banks typically don't issue credit cards to kids.

Digital Currency

Digital currency is a type of money that is unlike coins, checks, or paper money. It exists only online and has no physical form you can touch. It's like money that lives inside a computer.

Instead of being accounted for and transferred through banks like traditional money, digital currency uses electronic codes stored in computers. So, when you use a digital currency, it's all happening electronically.

DID YOU KNOW? *Most of the money we use today exists in the form of electronic money or numbers on a screen, stored electronically in banks or online accounts. If everyone tried to take out all their money as physical cash, the banks would quickly run out of money. So, even traditional money is a form of digital money.*

Other forms of digital money, such as cryptocurrencies, only exist on screens and computers. Cryptocurrencies like Bitcoin and Ethereum are examples of digital currencies that have no physical cash associated with them.

HOW MONEY IS USED IN EVERYDAY LIFE

Money is a standard tool of value that we use every day. It's essential because our economy—the system that tracks how people spend and earn money—is founded on the principles of money.

We use money to buy the things we need or want. This includes products (like toys, video games, and food) and services (like getting a haircut, seeing a dentist, or paying a builder).

But we don't always have to spend the money we earn as soon as we get it. It's also a good idea to save money. When you save money, you set it aside for the future. This could be to buy something bigger, like a bicycle, or to pay for any unexpected expenses, like buying a new video console if yours suddenly stops working. Or, it could be used to fund your retirement when you stop working later in life.

When you work, you earn money. Whether you do chores at home, like mowing the lawn or babysitting, or a full-time job when you get older, you earn money in exchange for your hard work. Once you've earned money, you decide how to spend it (or save it) on the things you need, such as food, clothes, a car, and a house. You wouldn't survive if you couldn't buy the stuff you needed.

Money makes the world go round. If people stopped spending, stores would have to close and people would lose their jobs and wouldn't have money to spend. That's why a healthy economy is a bit like a see-saw. It's about having a good balance between saving money (for future needs) and spending money (to buy the things you need now and keep the economy going).

YOUR KNOWLEDGE ABOUT MONEY

Fill in the blanks:

1. What's another word for money ? ________________
2. Money is also known as a ________________
3. Money is issued by each country's ________________
4. What's another name for trading? ________________
5. What was created to solve the problems that resulted from trading? ________________
6. What are you charged if you don't pay off your balance on a credit card? ________________

Match the country with its currency:

Mexico	$ Dollar
India	₱ Peso
United States	₹ Rupee
United Kingdom	¥ Yen
Japan	£ Pound

Circle the Correct Answer:

1. Which currency exists only online?

   Credit Card Debit Card Check Digital Currency

2. Which card is used to buy things now and pay for them later?

   Debit card Credit card

3. Which card deducts money directly from your bank account?

   Credit card Debit card

CHAPTER 2:

HOW TO EARN MONEY

To save and spend money, first, you must earn it.

WHY IT'S IMPORTANT TO START EARNING MONEY AT A YOUNG AGE

It's often only when you really want something, like a cool Lego set or craft kit that your parents won't buy for you, that you start thinking about earning money. But wouldn't it be great to have your own money to buy it immediately?

That's why starting earning money as early as possible is a good idea. When you earn your own money, you can save it up for the things you want in the future. You can also save up for even bigger things, like your very first car!

There are many benefits to earning money at a young age.

❶ Building a Strong Work Ethic

Earning money at a young age builds a strong work ethic. A work ethic is the set of values that you set for yourself in the workplace. It's how you behave while performing your work.

For example, a strong work ethic involves:

- Working hard to make something the best it can be
- Checking for mistakes
- Submitting work on time
- Helping others
- Showing up for work on time
- Staying focused
- Working well with others

❷ Learning the Value of Money

When you earn money, you begin to understand its value. Everything has value and is worth something. The effort and time you put into work produces value in the form of money.

> *For example, if you want a scooter that costs $89, you will have to work and earn at least $89 to pay for it.*

In this case, you exchange your hard-earned money ($89) for the item. This helps you understand and appreciate the value of money and the work required to earn it.

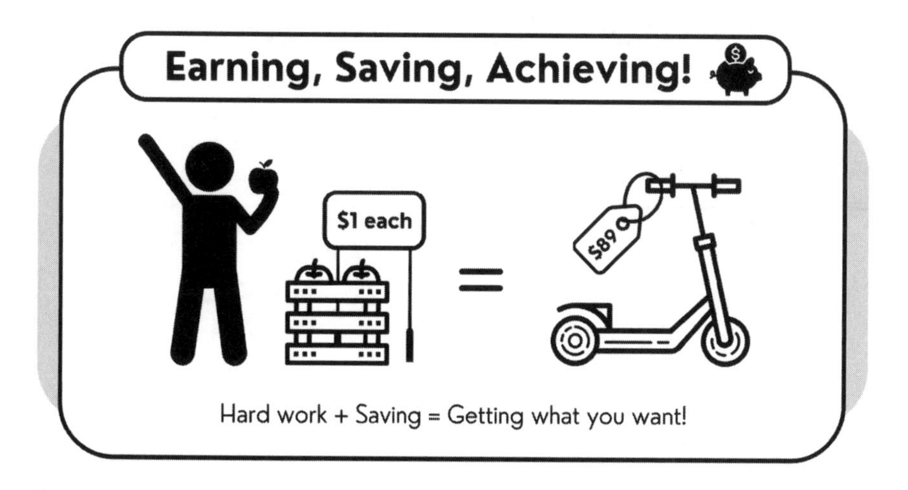

❸ Developing Communication Skills

Earning money teaches you how to communicate with different people outside school or at home. Communication at work may be different from what you are used to. It usually requires a more formal and professional approach.

You'll gain experience working with people of different backgrounds, ages, races, and personalities, and this will teach you how to interact and communicate with all types of people.

❹ Developing Problem-Solving Skills

Earning money teaches you how to solve problems and work well with others.

For example, say you have a book to sell for $5. The person buying the book hands you a $20 bill. How much change do you give back?

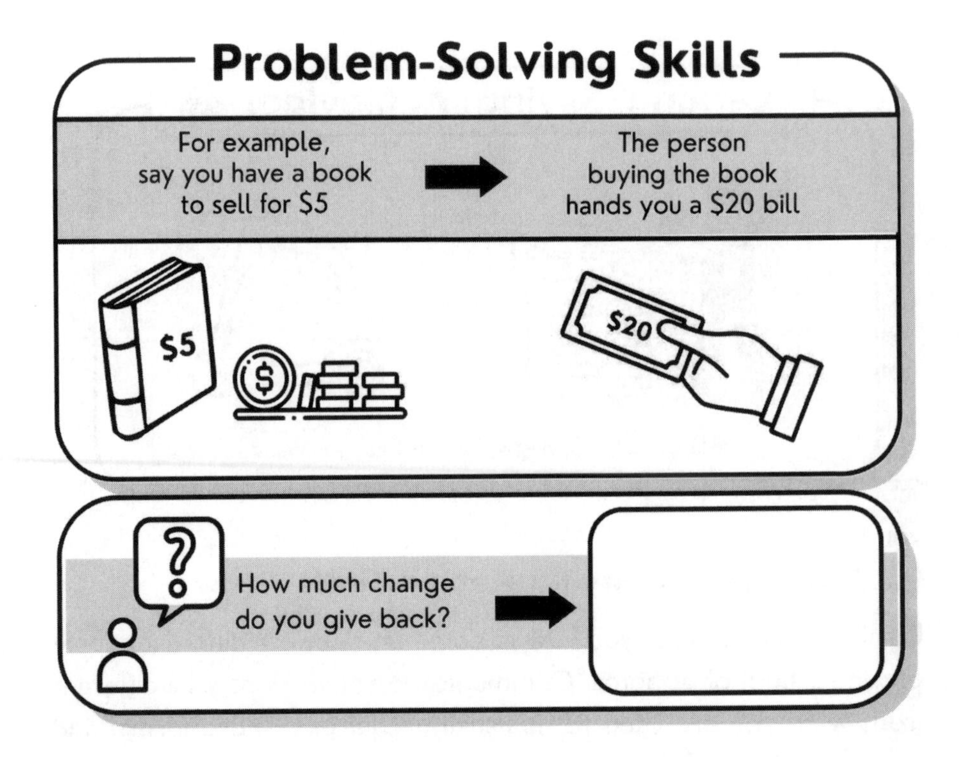

In this instance, you're learning how to handle money and how much change to give back.

5 Developing Teamwork

It's never too early to learn how to work as a team. Earning money will give you experience working with others, helping each other, relying on each other, and learning from each other to achieve a goal—not for yourself, but for a group of people.

6 Building Your Resume

Earning money and gaining work experience helps you develop skills that can benefit your future. It may help you get a scholarship for college or land your first job after high school. Having skills and work experience also sets you apart from others and shows your willingness to take on responsibilities.

❼ Understanding the World of Work

Earning money at a young age helps you discover what you do and don't enjoy about work. It begins to shape what you might want or not want from a future job.

Early exposure to various work settings and experiences will make you more comfortable and confident in the working environment when you are older.

❽ Understanding the Cost of Living

Earning money gives you a sense of how much things cost and the effort required to afford the things you need or want. It helps make you more responsible about spending money.

It feels great to earn your own money and purchase the things you want without depending on someone else to buy them. Making money at a young age helps you learn to be responsible with your money. This way, when you are older, you can do the things you want without worrying about how to pay for them.

Developing good habits of earning and managing money when you're young makes your life easier and more fulfilling as you get older.

WAYS TO EARN MONEY

Money certainly doesn't grow on trees. If it did, we wouldn't have to work and would all be rich! Earning money comes from hard work, but there are plenty of opportunities to make money, even at a young age.

Here are some ways to earn money when you're a kid:

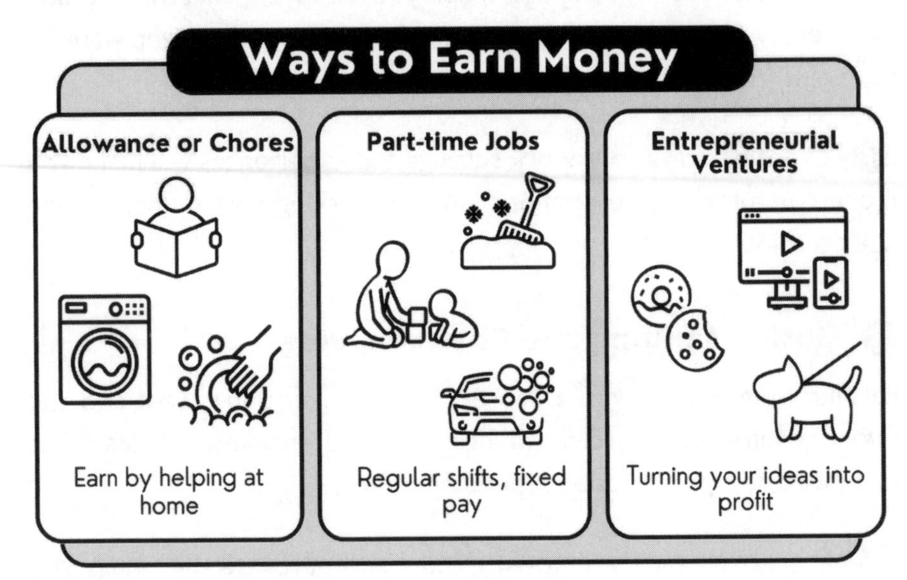

❶ Allowance or Chores

You can earn money by receiving an allowance for doing chores around the house or getting good grades in school.

> *For example, your parents might agree to give you $10 a week for doing the dishes, taking out the trash, doing the laundry, cleaning a particular area of the house, feeding the dog or cat, or keeping your grades at a B or above.*

❷ Part-Time Jobs

You can also make money by doing part-time jobs.

> *For example, you can babysit, mow lawns, rake leaves, shovel snow, or wash cars for people in your neighborhood.*

You could also get a part-time job in a cafe or restaurant when you're older.

❸ Entrepreneurial Ventures

Another way to make money is by starting a small business based on your hobbies and interests. This is called an entrepreneurial venture.

> *For example, you could create crafts or make items to sell, offer pet-sitting or dog-walking services to your neighbors, or bake and sell delicious treats.*

This is a fun way to turn your passions into a profitable venture and earn money doing what you love.

> **DID YOU KNOW?** *Some professional video gamers make millions of dollars by competing in e-sports tournaments. They play video games at a high level and earn money from prize pools, sponsorships, and streaming their gameplay online.*

PASSIVE INCOME – HOW TO EARN MONEY WHILE YOU SLEEP

Wouldn't it be great to make money even while you're sleeping? Believe it or not, there's something called passive income that allows people to do just that.

Passive income is money that you earn without actively working for it. It's like a money-making machine that keeps running, even when you're not actively involved.

There are lots of different ways to earn passive income. Some examples include owning a rental property, writing a book that continues to sell, or making an app that keeps getting downloaded. All these sources of income require lots of hard work and effort up front, but once they're set up and take off, they can make money regularly.

Let's look at the example of Ryan.

Ryan is a 7-year-old boy who has become a millionaire by reviewing toys on YouTube. Every time someone watches one of his videos, he earns a small percentage of the advertising money YouTube generates from his videos. The more viewers he has, the more money he makes.

Let's say he earns $0.003 every time someone views his video, and it gets 1,000 views. In this case, he would make $3.

1,000 x $0.003 = $3

Now imagine he gets a million views. He would make $3,000.

1,000,000 x $0.003 = $3,000

What makes this form of passive income so unique is that Ryan has built a loyal following of viewers. Whenever he uploads a new video, people watch it because they enjoy his content. And since his fans come from all over the world, Ryan continues to earn money even when he's fast asleep!

But Ryan's success didn't happen overnight. It took time, effort, and creating content that people enjoyed.

Passive income is a great way to earn money because it enables you to make money even when you're not actively working. However, it's essential to know that it isn't easy. Launching successful passive income business ventures takes dedication, time, and a lot of hard work. But the rewards can be worth it, as it can provide you with financial freedom. This may be something you want to explore as you get older.

HOW TO TURN A MONEY-MAKING IDEA INTO A REALITY

If you're ready to venture out and start your own business, a few steps are involved in the process.

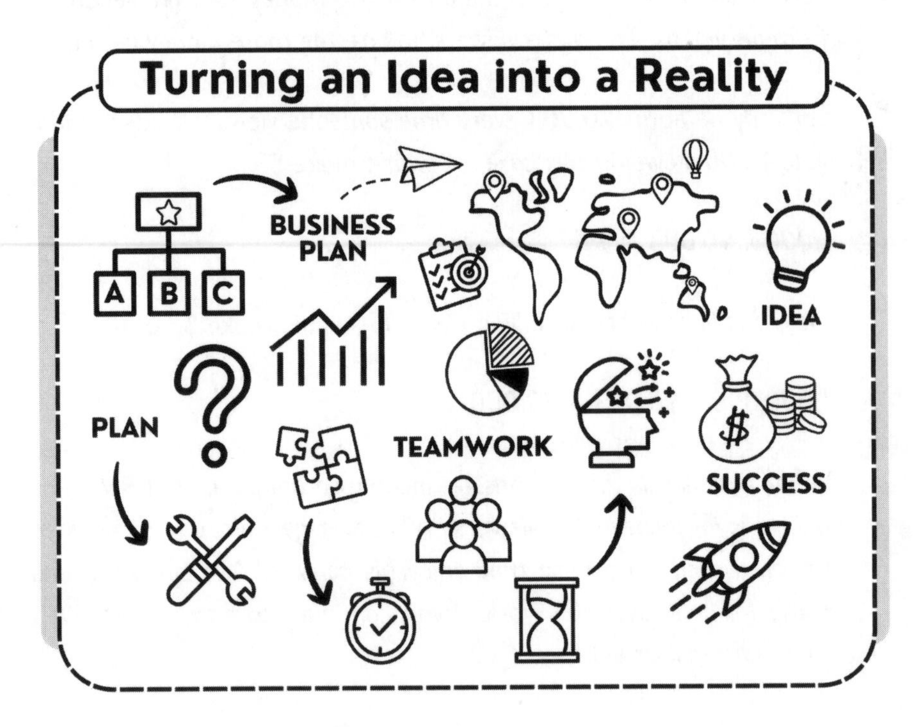

1 Come up with an idea.

Think about something you enjoy doing and that you can really get excited about. Start with something simple, like baking and selling cookies.

2 Conduct market research.

Think about who your customers will be. Everyone likes cookies, so they could be neighbors, friends, teachers, or just about anybody!

Also, think about who your competition will be. Is anyone else selling homemade cookies near you, and how is their business doing? This will tell you if there is a market for what you sell (for example, homemade cookies) and how successful your business could be. What kind of cookies do they sell, and how much do they charge?

3 Find something to make you stand out.

Find something that will set you apart from your competition.

> *For example, you could sell a type of cookie that no one else sells, or you could sell cookies as "sandwiches" and have vanilla or chocolate icing in the middle of two cookies.*

It's important to develop something to differentiate your cookies from those of your competitors.

4 Create a business plan.

Write your business plan. A business plan is like a roadmap for your business, guiding you and keeping you on track for success.

Your business plan should include the following:

- Who you are
- Your experience
- What product or service you're going to sell
- Your target customers
- The research you've compiled on your competitors and how you'll differentiate yourself from them
- How will you advertise and sell your product

- An estimate of sales, expenses, and profit
- Next steps and milestones
- Future goals

5 Get the word out.

Once you've created your business plan, it's time to get the word out and start selling. How are you going to market your business? Think of ways to promote your product or services. Will you advertise on social media, create flyers, or focus on word of mouth?

For example, if you created a cookie business, you could start by telling everyone you know. You could put flyers in schools or local businesses and use social media platforms to spread the word.

***DID YOU KNOW?** The game "Among Us" became super popular among kids and teens because of word of mouth. It started with a small group of players who loved the game and shared their excitement with their friends. Soon, everyone wanted to play, and it became a massive sensation because people talked about it and recommended it to others!*

UNDERSTANDING PROFIT

Once you've come up with your own money-making idea, you must understand the fundamentals of profit before you can turn it into a reality. Most businesses exist to make money, so understanding profit is critical to any new venture.

Profit is the money you make when you sell your products or services, after you take away the expenses, like materials, labor, and other overhead costs.

For instance, imagine you're selling homemade jewelry. The profit is the money that remains after you pay for the materials, such as beads, bracelets, or chains.

So, if each necklace costs you $10 in materials and you sell them for $20, your profit is $10 per necklace. However, it's important to remember that materials aren't your only costs when you make your own products. You must also include overhead costs like labor, advertising, and electricity.

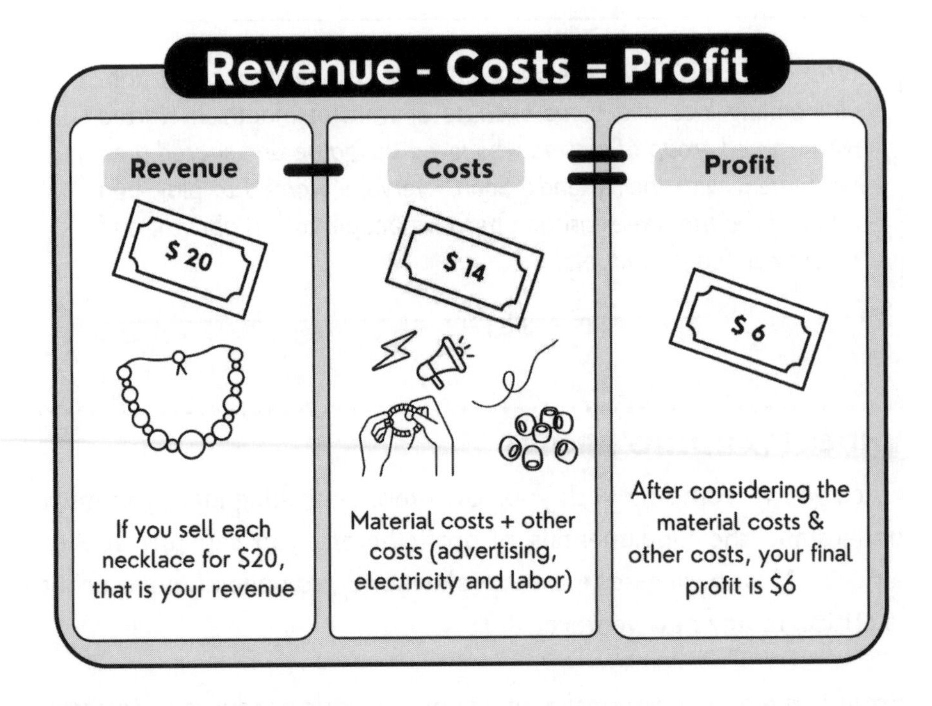

By ensuring your revenue exceeds your costs, you can create a positive profit and make money! A clear understanding of profit will help you manage your costs and take the next steps to turn your money-making idea into a reality.

HOW TO GET A PART-TIME JOB

Another way to earn money is to get a part-time or full-time job. Part-time jobs are often available to teenagers or students looking to gain work experience and earn some extra cash. These jobs include working at a local store, restaurant, or cafe.

Here are the steps it takes to get your first part-time job.

❶ Determine your interests and strengths.

Think of something you're interested in, good at, or enjoy doing.

For example, suppose you're interested in food and enjoy meeting new people. In that case, you might consider working in a cafe.

❷ Search for job openings.

To find out who is hiring, list all the cafes near you. Call each cafe and ask if they are hiring, or stop by and ask them in person.

❸ Prepare a resume.

Once you find out who is hiring, you need to prepare and submit a resume. A resume is a document that outlines your skills, work experience, education, and achievements.

A resume includes the following information:

- Name
- Address
- Phone number
- Email address
- Objective—A short description of yourself and your goals
- Work experience—Any jobs or volunteer work you've had
- Your education—The name and address of your school, your grades, and any coursework that ties in with the job you are applying for
- Additional skills

Here is an example of a resume:

Example Resume

Jane Doe

123 Main Street Anytown, CA 12345
(123) 456-7890 | jane.doe@email.com

About Me

I am a friendly, organized High School Student looking for part-time work in retail. I love learning new skills, and working in a team.

Experience

Assisitant, ABC Cafe **July - Dec 2023**

- Serving coffee at local cafe
- Valuable experience in customer service

Babysitting **Jan - Dec 2023**

- Babysitting for children aged 3-9, in my local area

Education

High School Senior **Class of 2023**
Anytown High School, Anytown, CA

Awards

- National Honor Society
- President's List
- AP Scholar with Distinction

Skills

- Experience using cash & credit payments
- Serving customers food & drink
- Excellent communication skills
- Strong organizational & time management skills

Interests

I am captain of the school basketball team, and I also play lacrosse. I have a passion for travel and speak Spanish fluently.

❹ Interview

If the cafe you're applying to likes your resume, they may invite you in for an interview. In an interview, someone from the cafe will sit down and talk with you, face to face. They may ask about your experience and why you want to work there. You should always be polite and answer all questions honestly.

The best way to earn money is to work hard. Hard work always pays off. It shows employers that you are responsible and motivated, and that you take pride in your work.

With the money you earn from working, you can now buy what you need and want.

CREATE YOUR OWN BUSINESS IDEA

Think of a fun business idea that you would like to turn into a reality. It could be a product (like baking cookies) or service (like walking dogs.)

YOUR BIG IDEA

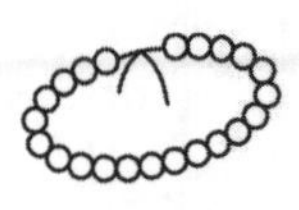

a. What will you sell or offer? [Your Product or Service]

____

b. What makes it unique?

____

c. What is the main goal of your business?

☐ Make money ☐ Help others ☐ Have fun

MARKETING

a. Who are your customers (kids, parents, etc.)? [Target customers]

____

____

____

b. How will you let people know about your business? Will you make posters, create a website, or tell your friends? [Promotion ideas]

____

c. What will your business be called? [Business name]

____

d. Create a unique logo or symbol for your business. Think about colors, shapes, and images that represent your business. [Logo design]

FINANCES

a. How much money do you need to start your business?

____

b. How much will it cost to make each product or provide your service?

____

c. How much will you charge for your product or service?

____

d. What will be your profit? How much will you make after you take out your costs?

____

Remember, this activity is all about using your imagination and having fun. Fill in the gaps with your creative ideas for your own business. You can also discuss your ideas with friends and family for feedback and support. Have fun being an entrepreneur!

CHAPTER 3:

HOW TO SAVE MONEY

Once you've earned money, you can save or spend it. Let's start by talking about the importance of saving money. Saving is when you set aside a portion of your money for the future.

THE IMPORTANCE OF SAVING

Saving money is an important habit to develop, especially when you've worked hard to earn it. By setting aside a portion of your earnings each month, you can achieve your future goals and afford things that you may not be able to afford right now.

> *For example, imagine you want to buy a new pair of shoes that cost $200, but you currently have only $50. To reach your goal, you'll need to save $150. It's essential to plan how much money you can set aside each month to reach your savings target.*
>
> *If you can save at least $30 per month, it would take you five months to save $150. When you combine this amount with the $50 you already have, you'll have a total of $200, which is enough to buy the shoes.*

Saving Money Allows You to Put It Aside for Emergencies

While it's good to set aside money for things you want or need, it's also good to have money set aside for unexpected emergencies.

Suppose you have a pet dog, and your parents agreed to let you have it on the condition that you take care of all its expenses. Suddenly, your dog starts limping and requires veterinary care. If you've regularly set aside money each month, you will have the funds to take your dog to the vet immediately.

If your dog has a broken leg or any other health issue, it's crucial to get professional help as soon as possible. This is why it is essential to save money. Otherwise, you might have to borrow money from someone else or delay the necessary medical treatment for your dog, which isn't the best option for your furry friend.

By saving money, you can be prepared for unexpected situations and ensure your beloved pet receives the care it needs promptly.

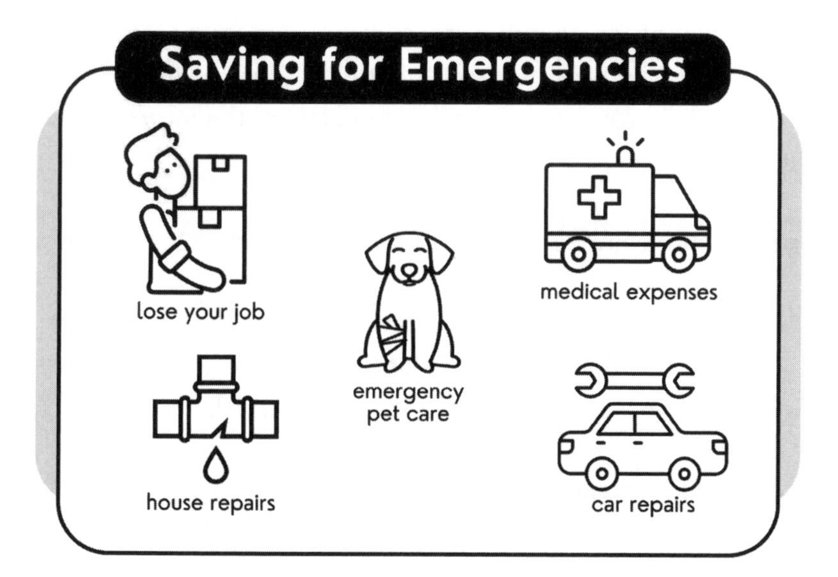

Saving Money in a Bank Earns You Interest

When you deposit money into a savings account at the bank, the bank pays you for keeping it there. This is called interest.

Interest is like a reward for saving your money. It's usually a percentage of the amount you have held at the bank.

For example, let's say you have $100 in a savings account, and the bank agrees to pay you an interest rate of 4% yearly. That means they'll give you $4 as interest at the end of the year.

To calculate interest, you can use a simple formula: Multiply the amount you have saved ($100) by the interest rate (0.04, which is the decimal equivalent of 4%).

So $100 X 0.04 = $4.00

There is also another type of interest called compound interest. Compound interest is interest earned on interest. This means you not only make interest on your initial deposit, but also on the interest you have already earned.

Using the same example, let's see how compound interest works.

In the first year, you had $100 in your savings account, and the bank paid you $4.00 in interest (4% of $100). At the end of the first year, your savings account has grown to $104.00 ($100 + $4.00).

Now, in the second year, you earn interest not only on your initial $100, but also on the interest you earned in the first year. Using the same interest rate of 4%, you would earn $4.16 in interest (4% of $104). By the end of the second year, your savings account would have increased to $108.16 ($104 + $4.16).

Do you see how the interest went from $4.00 in the first year to $4.16 in the second year? This is because you earned interest on top of the interest you made the previous year.

This cycle of earning interest on the initial amount plus the interest continues year after year, making your savings grow faster. It's like a snowball rolling down a hill that grows bigger and bigger each year. The more money you deposit, the more interest you earn; the longer you leave it in the account, the faster it grows.

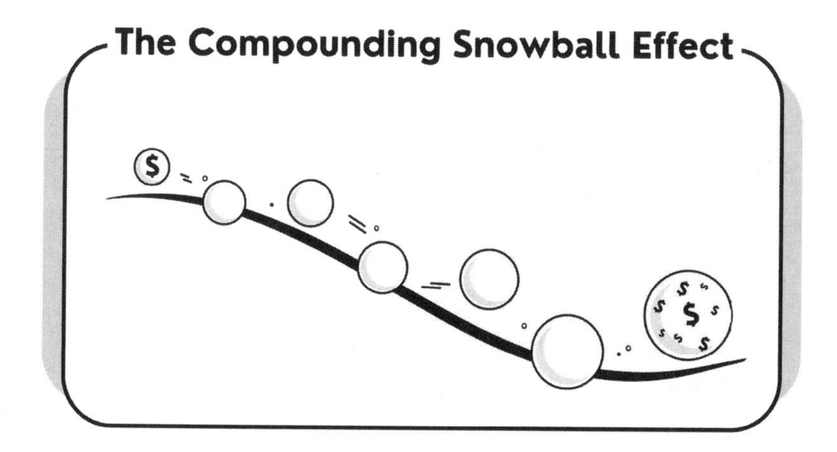

This is why it's important to start saving early and to regularly add to your savings. It allows your money to work for you and grow over time.

Did you know that if you saved just $1 every day starting at the age of 10 and let it grow with a 5% interest rate, by the time you were 18, you would have around $3,600? And if you continued saving until you were 25, you will have about $8,000! The power of starting early and letting compound interest work its magic can make your money grow over time.

HOW TO SET SAVINGS GOALS

To keep yourself motivated and have a clear target to work towards, it's helpful to set goals when saving money. An excellent way to set effective goals is to remember the word "SMART."

S = Specific (What exactly are you saving for?)
M = Measurable (How much do you need to save?)
A = Achievable (Is your goal realistic and achievable?)
R = Relevant (Why is this goal important to you?)
T = Time-bound (How long will it take you to achieve your goal?)

Let's say you have your heart set on getting a new bike. You're really excited about riding around on your own wheels. Setting a savings goal for buying a bike gives you a strong motivation to save more and save faster. You'll do your best to set aside as much money as possible in a shorter amount of time so you can get that bike sooner.

Here's how you can save using the SMART saving method:

S = Specific: Save money for a new bike.
M = Measurable: Determine how much the bike costs and how much you need to save.
A = Achievable: Set a goal that you can realistically reach.
R = Relevant: Understand why getting the bike is essential to you.
T = Time-bound: Decide when you want to reach your savings goal.

For example, if the bike you want costs $200, you can set a goal of saving $20 each week. In 10 weeks, you'll have enough money to buy the bike.

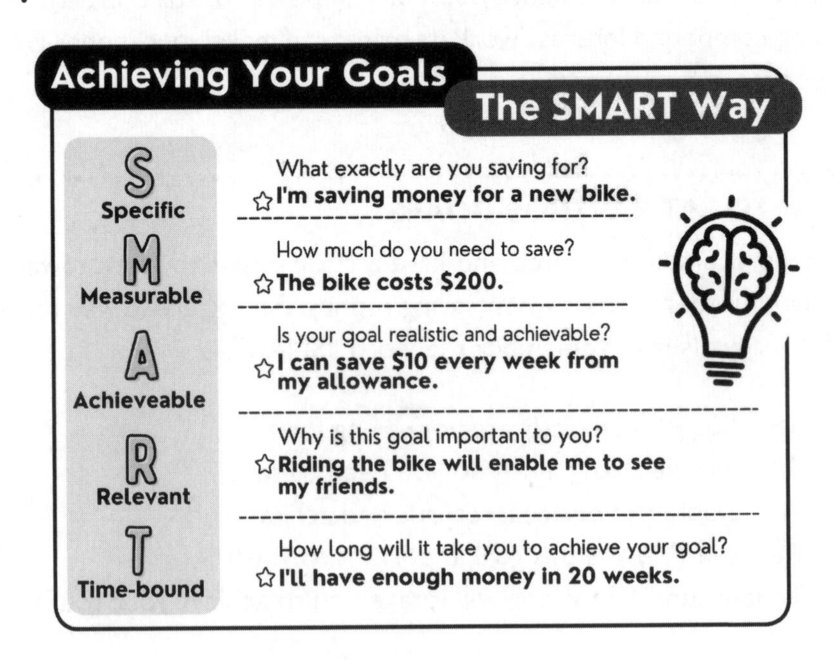

Remember, using the SMART saving method, you can easily set savings goals and buy what you want over time.

When it comes to savings goals, they can be categorized into different timeframes:

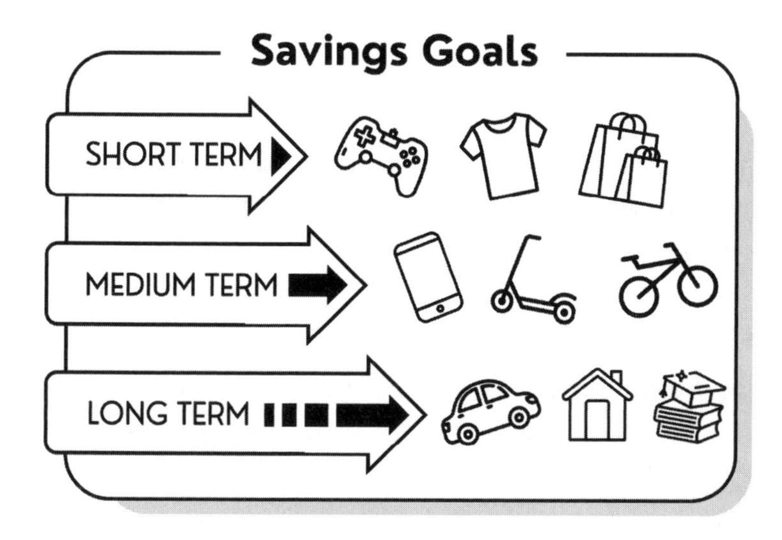

Short-Term Savings Goals

These are goals that can usually be reached within weeks or months. An example is saving up to buy a toy or a new video game.

Medium-Term Savings Goals

These goals usually take about a year to accomplish. An example is saving for a bike or a scooter.

Long-Term Savings Goals

These are goals that require several years of saving to achieve. Examples include saving for college tuition or a car.

By setting SMART savings goals and categorizing them based on their timeframes, you'll have a clear roadmap to follow and a sense of accomplishment as you reach each milestone. Remember, saving money is a journey. Setting goals can make it an exciting and rewarding adventure!

HOW TO SAVE MONEY

Saving money is a great habit to develop, and there are several ways to reach your savings goals. You just need to find the method that works best for you.

Here are a few methods you can try:

- **Piggy bank:** Start by regularly putting a small amount of money aside into a piggy bank. While it won't earn you interest, seeing your piggy bank fill as you keep adding more money is fun.
- **Savings account:** Open a savings account at a bank. This is a great way to keep your money safe and earn interest on your savings.
- **Savings app or online saver:** Explore different savings apps or online platforms to help you save towards your goals. These tools often offer interest and allow you to set savings goals so you can track your progress. Some even automate your savings so you can put a small amount into your account regularly.

Different Methods to Save

Piggy Bank

A simple way to save money

Savings Account

Keeps your money safe while earning interest

Savings App or Online Saver

A simple way to save online

Remember, finding the saving method that suits you best will make it easier and more enjoyable to reach your savings goals. Start saving today and watch your money grow!

HOW TO OPEN A SAVINGS ACCOUNT

When you start earning money, having a safe place to keep it is crucial. A savings account at a bank is a secure place to deposit and store your money while earning interest over time.

Here are some things to consider when choosing the best bank for your savings account:

- **Convenience:** Look for a bank that is easy to access whenever you need to deposit or withdraw money.
- **Customer service:** Make sure the staff at the bank are friendly, helpful, and knowledgeable and that you are comfortable dealing with them.

- **Fees:** Some banks charge fees to manage your account. Check what expenses the bank charges on your savings account, such as maintenance fees for falling below a minimum balance. Shop around for banks with fewer and lower fees so you can keep more of your savings.
- **Interest rates:** Different banks offer different interest rates. Look for the bank with the highest interest rate to help your savings grow faster.

Once you've chosen a bank, it's time to open your account. Some banks require you to do this in person, while others allow you to do it online.

Step 1: Fill out an application.

The bank will first ask you to complete an application with your name, address, and other personal details. Once the application is filled out, you must sign it to show that you agree to their policies and that the information you gave them is correct. If you're under 18, you may also need a parent or guardian to sign.

Step 2: Provide identification.

Next, you may need to provide identification, such as your birth certificate, school ID, or passport, to prove your identity. This is a requirement, as the bank wants to be sure you are who you say you are.

Step 3: Make an initial deposit.

In most cases, you must deposit a minimum amount of money into your new savings account to activate the account. Remember, you may need to keep a minimum amount in your savings account to avoid a fee.

Step 4: Deposit and withdraw money.

Once the account is opened, you can deposit and withdraw money. There are three ways you can handle transactions that involve your account.

1. **In person at the bank:** Fill out a deposit or withdrawal slip at the bank. Hand it to the bank teller, and they will process your transaction.

2. **At an ATM:** Some banks issue bank cards with your name and account number. You can use these cards at ATMs. Set a PIN number for your card to ensure security. At the ATM, insert your bank card, enter your PIN number, select whether you want to

make a deposit or withdrawal, and enter the amount. Once the transaction is complete, remove your card and keep the receipt for your records. Note that some banks may charge a fee for ATM transactions.

3. **Online:** Most banks offer online banking or mobile apps. Set up an online account with your bank. Once logged in, you can deposit and transfer money using the bank's website or app. You can even deposit checks by taking a picture using a phone.

THE SAVINGS GOAL THERMOMETER

INSTRUCTIONS

1 Think about what you want to save for:

This should be something you really want. It could be a toy, book, game, or even a fun day out. Remember, it should be something you'll need to save up for over a little while.

2 Write your goal at the top of the thermometer:

At the top of the thermometer, write down what you're saving for and how much it costs.

3 Break down your goals into smaller steps:

If you're saving $100, you could break it down into four $25 steps. Write down each step on the thermometer from bottom to top.

4 Track your progress:

Each time you save some money, color in your thermometer up to that level of your savings.

5 Keep going until you reach your goal:

It may take some time, but stick with it, and before you know it, you'll have your thermometer all colored in, and you'll have reached your goal.

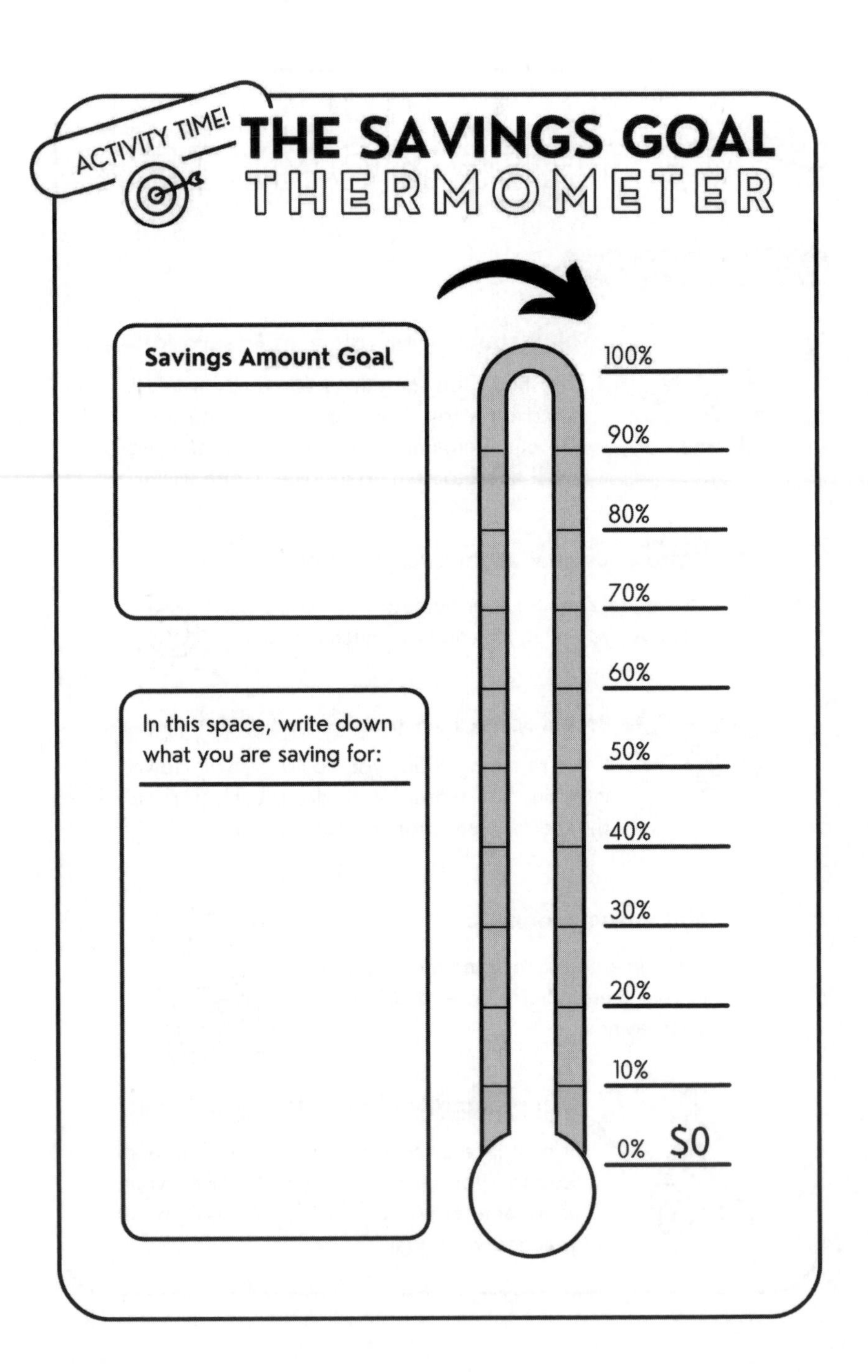
ACTIVITY TIME!
THE SAVINGS GOAL
THERMOMETER
Savings Amount Goal
In this space, write down what you are saving for:
100%
90%
80%
70%
60%
50%
40%
30%
20%
10%
0% $0

CHAPTER 4:

HOW TO SPEND MONEY WISELY

Now that you have a good idea about how to save money let's talk about spending money wisely.

Just because you have money doesn't mean you should go out and spend it all! It's essential to think carefully about what you are spending your money on and whether it is something you need. You might feel like you need a new game console, but is that a need? Or do you just want it because your friends have one? Let's look at needs and wants to help you make smart choices.

NEEDS VS. WANTS

- **Needs:** These are necessary for our survival and well-being, and we cannot live without them. Examples include food, clothes, water, and shelter.
- **Wants:** These are non-essential items and things we would like to have because they make life more enjoyable.

For example, if your shoes are worn out and don't fit you properly anymore, you need a new pair to protect your feet and walk comfortably. However, wanting a new video game just because your friends have it is a want, not a necessity.

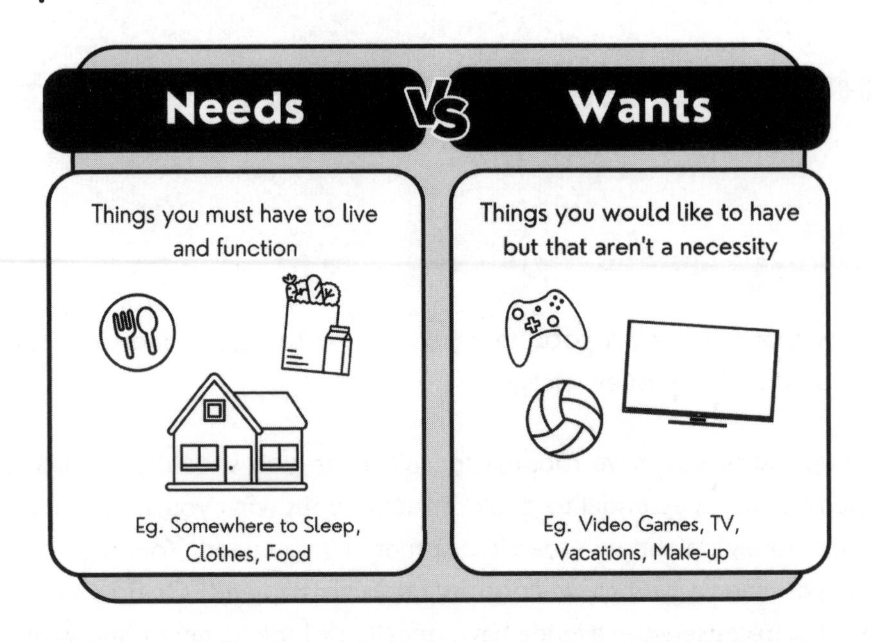

It's important to prioritize spending your money on needs before wants. Before you make a purchase, consider whether it's something you genuinely need. Ask yourself, "Is this something I really need to survive?" If the answer is no and you can wait a little while, it's not an immediate need, but more of a want.

Remember, it's okay to have wants—we all need fun and downtime. But it is important to make smart choices and spend money wisely.

HOW TO UNDERSTAND THE CONCEPT OF VALUE

Understanding the concept of value is essential when deciding how to spend your hard-earned money. Value refers to how much something is worth and what you get in return for what you pay.

When you think of value, there are a few things to consider:

1. **Utility:** How much use will you get from the item? Will it do its job or make you happy?
2. **Quality:** How long will the item last? Will it last a long time or wear out quickly?
3. **Price:** How much does it cost? Is it affordable?

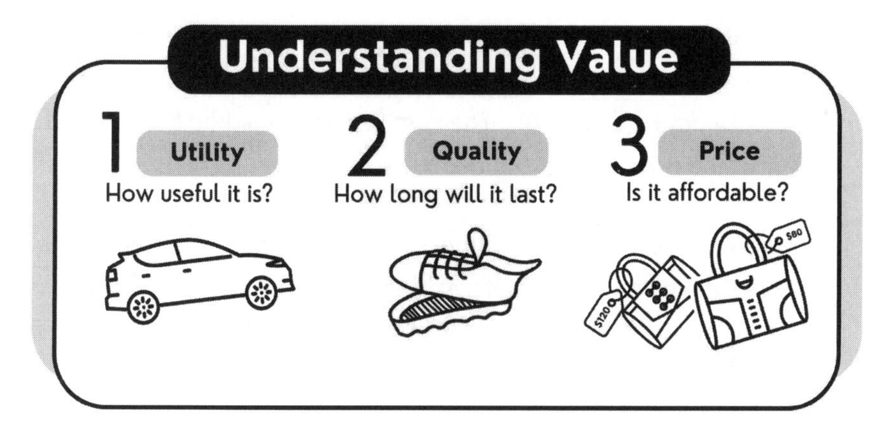

Considering these factors can help you decide whether something is worth buying. Remember, lower prices don't always represent better value.

For example, let's say you need a new pair of shoes. You find two options—one that costs $175 and another that costs $50. On the *face of it, the $50 pair seems like a better deal because they are cheaper. But let's consider quality and cost per use.*

The $175 shoes are made with superior materials and are built to last. On the other hand, the $50 pair uses low-quality materials that won't last as long.

Now let's consider the cost per use.

If the more expensive pair last for two years and you wear them daily, you've worn them around 730 times (365 days x 2 years). So the cost per use would be $175 divided by 730, which is approximately $0.24 per use.

In comparison, if the $50 shoes last only six months before wearing out and you wear them every day, that would be approximately 180 uses (30 days x 6 months). The cost per use would be $50 divided by 180, which is roughly $0.28 per use.

In this example, even though the $175 shoes are more expensive, they are better value in the long term, as they last longer and have a lower cost per use. Sometimes, buying higher-quality items that last longer can save you money.

Of course, once you have decided on the product you want to buy, it's always worth hunting for sales and discounts. You might be able to get those same shoes for $150 if you shop around.

Finally, it's also worth remembering that value is personal and can extend beyond how much something is worth. *For instance, a wooden toy made by your grandfather might not be worth anything on the market, but its sentimental value to you could be priceless.*

HOW TO MAKE WISE CHOICES WHEN SPENDING MONEY ONLINE

Spending money online can be convenient and easy. In just a few clicks, you can buy almost anything you want. However, just because you can buy something doesn't mean you should!

As with any purchase, when spending money online, it's essential to ensure you are only buying what you need and getting the best deal possible.

Here are a few tips to help you spend money online wisely:

- **Always ask your parents**: Before making a purchase, ask your parents or an adult if it is okay.
- **Do your research**: Before making a purchase, do your research to ensure the item does what you need.
- **Read reviews:** Read customer reviews to find out what others think and to get an idea of how the item performs. Look out for red flags or repeated problems. If there are many negative reviews, it may be worth considering a different option.
- **Compare prices:** Once you know the exact make and model of the item, compare prices to ensure you are getting the best deal.
- **Be aware of hidden costs:** Look out for delivery costs, taxes, and other fees that can add up.
- **Check the returns policy:** If the item doesn't meet your expectations, can you return it quickly without being charged?
- **Only buy from trustworthy websites:** This is the most important rule when buying anything online. Are you familiar with the site? Have you heard of it before? Before giving credit card information

to any website, you should consider these things. If you're unsure, ask your parents or an adult for help.

- **Look out for sales:** Try to buy items on sale, since this is a great way to get something you want while spending less money.
- **Look for coupon codes:** You can often find discounts and coupons online. Be sure to check for these before you make a purchase.
- **Buy used:** Used items are often as good as new items, but cost less. There are often bargains to be found at garage sales and thrift stores. You can also find great deals on second-hand items on sites like eBay, Craigslist, and Facebook Marketplace.
- **Be patient:** If you can wait to buy something, you might be able to get it at a lower price or find a better deal.

Following these tips can teach you to spend money wisely online. If you take the time, you can find great deals and save money on the things you want to buy.

Remember, the best way to save money is to avoid spending it in the first place!

HOW TO PAY FOR THINGS ONLINE AND IN STORE

Once you've decided what you want to buy, you need to be able to pay for it using a digital payment method.

DID YOU KNOW? *In the United States, over 80% of adults make online payments for their purchases. That means the majority of people use digital methods like credit cards, mobile payment apps, or online banking to pay for goods and services.*

Understanding Credit Cards, Debit Cards, and Buy Now Pay Later

When you make purchases online or in stores, you have the option to pay with a credit or debit card. What are these cards, and how do they work?

CREDIT CARD, DEBIT CARD, AND BUY NOW PAY LATER

	PROS	CONS
CREDIT CARDS	• Useful for big purchases • Some cards give you rewards	• May encourage more spending • High interest rates if not paid back on time • Bad credit can hurt
DEBIT CARDS	• Can't go into debt • Don't have to carry lots of cash	• Easy to use, may encourage spending • Comes straight out of the account
BUY NOW PAY LATER	• Spreads payments over time • Easy to set up and use	• High interest if instalments are late • Encourages more spending

Credit Cards

Credit cards are a type of loan. This means that every time you use a credit card, you borrow money from the bank or card supplier. You will have to repay this money with interest.

Interest is the fee the bank or card supplier charges you for lending you the money to make your purchase.

For example, say you spend $100 using your credit card, and the bank charges 10% interest. This means you owe the bank $110.

$100 x 0.10 = $10
$100 + $10 = $110

If you don't pay this back, the bank may charge you another 10% interest on the $110. Now, you owe the bank $121.

$110 x 0.10 = $11
$110 + $11 = $121

As you can see, the interest can quickly add up, and you can owe a lot of money to the bank. This is why you must be careful if you use a credit card and always pay off the balance every month.

DID YOU KNOW? *The first consumer credit card was introduced in 1958 by Bank of America. It was called the "BankAmericard" and it revolutionized how people could make purchases by allowing them to use credit. BankAmericard became known as VISA in 1976, and it's still widely used for making payments worldwide!*

Debit Cards

Debit cards are different from credit cards. When you use a debit card, the money is taken directly from your bank account.

This means you can only spend the money you have in your account. If you don't have the funds already deposited in your account, you won't be able to use your debit card. So, unlike a credit card, you cannot borrow money to make a purchase.

> *For example, say you have $100 in your bank account and use your debit card to make an online purchase of $50. The $50 is immediately taken from your account balance, leaving you with $50 in your account.*

If you try to spend more than you have in your account, the transaction will be declined.

Both credit and debit cards can be helpful for making purchases online. While they may look the same, they are very different and should be used with caution.

Here are a few things to keep in mind when using credit or debit cards:

- **Ask your parents:** Always ask your parent's permission before you use their cards.
- **Check your balance:** Check your balance regularly to know how much money you have in your account. This prevents you from spending more money than you have and helps you identify possible fraud on your account.
- **Stay on top of payments:** When you are older, if you get a credit card, ensure you understand the terms and conditions and stay on

top of your monthly payments. Interest can quickly add up, and you can end up owing a lot of money to the bank if you're not careful.

- **Keep it safe:** Keep your credit or debit card in a safe place. This will help prevent someone from stealing and using it without your permission.

Many apps now allow parents to control their child's spending. This can be a great way to help teach young adults about money and how to spend it wisely.

Buy Now Pay Later

You may have heard of "buy now, pay later." This relatively new payment option allows you to buy something today and pay for it in smaller installments over time. A lot of online websites offer their customers this payment option.

For example, suppose you want to buy a new jacket for $200. The website offers you the option to pay for it over three months. This means you would pay $66.67 per month for three months.

$200 ÷ 3 = $66.67

At the end of the three months, you would have paid off the jacket in full.

This may sound like a great idea at first, but there are some things you should know before you do this.

First, this is debt. This means you are borrowing money from the company to pay for the jacket.

Second, you will be charged interest if you don't pay on time. This means you will end up paying more than the original price.

For example, suppose you have three months to pay for your jacket. If you pay it all in those three months, there is no interest to pay. This is called "interest-free." But if you miss a payment and fail to pay it off in those three months and still owe $50, the company will charge you interest on the $50.

If the interest rate is 20%, your $50 debt would turn into a $60 debt.

$50 x 0.20 = $10
$50 + $10 = $60

So, while "buy now, pay later" might sound like a great idea, you should think carefully before using it. Be sure you can afford the monthly payments and that you will pay them off within the interest-free period.

TIP: If you need clarification on something, ask your parents or an adult you trust for help. They will be able to give you some good advice.

When shopping online, all it takes is a few clicks to make a purchase. Always review your purchase before confirming your order. Whether using a credit card, debit card, or cash, remember to think about what you are buying and why. By doing this, you can avoid making impulsive purchases that you may later regret.

AN INTRODUCTION TO BUDGETING

Budgeting is an important way to ensure you use your money wisely. It helps you plan and keep track of your spending so you can make smart decisions about your money in the future. This means looking at how much money you earn and determining how much you should save each month, as well as how much you can spend wisely.

For example, imagine you are saving up for a new pair of jeans that cost $100. You will need to work out how much money you have coming in each month and how much you can afford to put away until you have enough for the jeans.

Remember, saving any amount is better than saving nothing at all. Even if it's a small amount, putting money into savings regularly adds up over time. It's always good to set aside some money for the future, just in case you need it.

By budgeting, you can avoid debt, save up for things you want in the future, and have peace of mind knowing that you have money saved up for unexpected expenses. It's a smart way to manage your money and plan for a better financial future.

DIFFERENT WAYS TO BUDGET

There are various methods to help you learn to budget your money. Here are a couple of popular ones if you're just starting out:

1. **The Jar Method:** This method divides your money into different jars for different goals.

   For example, you might have a "new shoes" jar and a "new pet" jar.

Jar Method

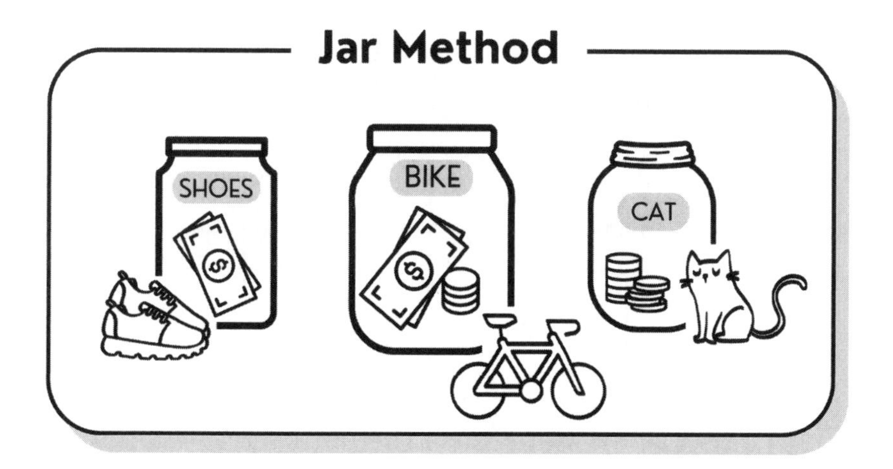

Every time you receive money, you put a portion into your jars. This can be a fun way to save, and also helps you see how much you are saving for each goal.

2. **The 50/30/20 Rule:** In this case, you divide your money into three categories: essentials, wants, and savings. You allocate 50% to essential expenses like food or clothes, 30% to things you want, like new toys or games, and 20% to savings.

For example, if you received $100 for your birthday, you would divide it up as follows:

$50 for essentials, such as food or clothes

$30 for wants, such as a new toy or video game

$20 for savings, which goes into a savings account

The **50/30/20 rule** is a good starting point, but you can adjust it depending on your income and expenses.

The 50/30/20 rule is a good starting point, but you can adjust it depending on your income and expenses.

There are many ways to budget, and finding a system that works for you is crucial. Always be mindful of your spending and try to put some money away each month into savings.

HOW TO AVOID IMPULSE PURCHASES

Sometimes, you might see something and feel you need to buy it right away. This is called an "impulse purchase." Impulse purchases are purchases you make without much thought or planning. It's easily done, especially when shopping online. If you're not careful, impulse purchases can quickly lead to spending more money than you have. So, it's essential to think carefully before you buy something.

Here are a few tips to avoid impulse buying:

- **Wait 24 hours:** Have a waiting period of 24 hours before making a large purchase. This gives you time to consider how much use it would get and if it is worth buying.
- **Avoid shopping when emotional:** Sometimes, feelings of boredom, sadness, or even happiness can lead to impulse purchases. This is sometimes called "retail therapy," where people shop to improve their mood. But it's usually not a good way to spend money.
- **Create a shopping list:** By focusing on the list, you can avoid getting distracted by non-essential items.

ACTIVITY: THE SUPERMARKET BUDGETING CHALLENGE

Get ready to be a party planner! In this activity, you'll learn about budgeting while planning a fun party for your friends. The catch? You only have $25 to spend.

Here's what to do:

1. **Imagine your party:** Decide how many friends to invite, what snacks to serve, and if you want decorations or games.
2. **Make a shopping list:** List the items you need, like snacks, drinks, and decorations. Remember, you only have $25.
3. **Estimate costs:** Check online or think about the store prices to estimate the cost of each item.
4. **Use your budgeting template:** Fill out the template on the next page. Write each item, estimated price, quantity, and total cost (PRICE x QUANTITY).
5. **Calculate your total:** Add the costs. If it's over $25, adjust your plan until it fits the budget.
6. **Finalize:** Stick to your final party plan!

Remember, this activity is about making smart choices to have fun while staying within your budget.

ACTIVITY TIME!

THE SUPERMARKET BUDGETING CHALLENGE

PARTY DATE

______

BUDGET:
$ ______

ITEM	PRICE	QUANTITY	TOTAL COST
Example Mango	$2	2 pcs	$4
TOTAL SPENT			**$**

REMAINING BUDGET:
$ ______

CHAPTER 5:

HOW TO GIVE AND SHARE

Now that we've talked about saving and spending wisely, let's explore another important aspect of handling money: giving and sharing. It's not all about keeping money for yourself. Sometimes, the most valuable thing you can do with your money is to help others.

Whether it's donating to a charity, supporting a friend in need, or contributing to a cause you care about, giving can have a significant impact. It's a wonderful way to make a difference and bring joy to others.

THE JOY OF GIVING AND HELPING OTHERS

There's nothing better than giving, sharing, or helping those in need. People often confuse giving with money, but you don't have to be rich to make a difference in someone's life. Even the smallest gestures, like giving up your seat on a bus or opening the door for a stranger, can brighten someone's day and make the world a better place.

There are many ways to give and share without involving money. Volunteering your time, donating items, or helping others costs nothing, but are all valuable ways to make a difference in people's lives.

When you give or help others, it brings a sense of satisfaction, fulfillment, and joy.

> *For example, think about when you made a special gift for your parents and saw their happiness when they received it. That feeling of joy and satisfaction is priceless.*

The same goes for helping others without expecting anything in return. It provides a warm and fulfilling feeling inside, knowing that you've positively impacted someone's life.

Here are some examples of ways you can help others:

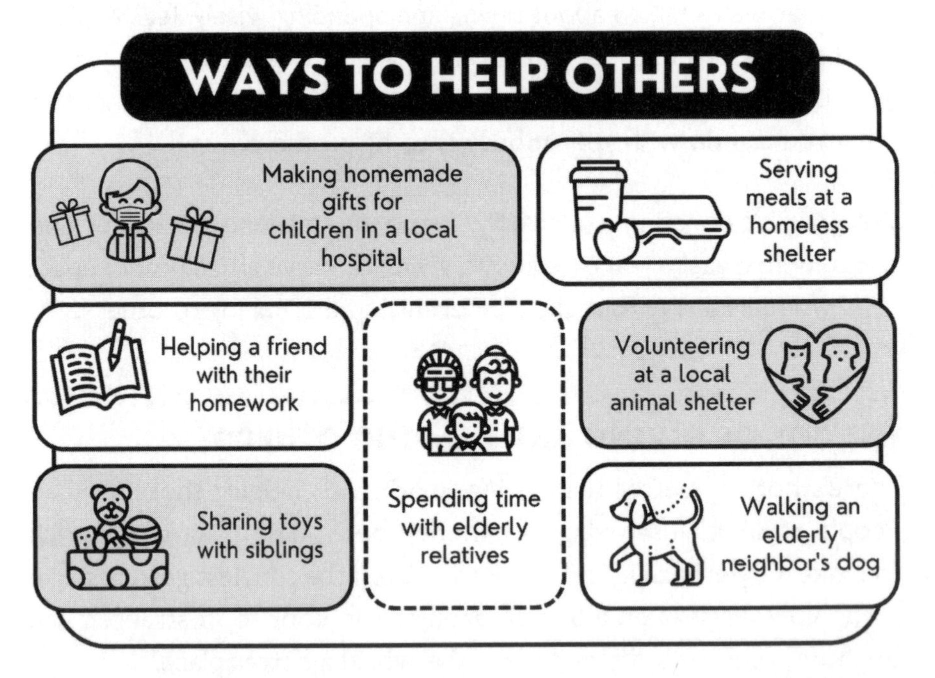

There are so many ways you can give and share. It's important to remember that even the smallest acts can bring joy to those on the receiving end and spread kindness and love.

UNDERSTANDING DONATIONS AND CHARITABLE GIVING

Giving can also involve making donations or giving to a charity.

Donations are a way of giving money, goods, or time to a cause or organization that helps others. It can be money, such as giving a portion of your monthly allowance, or it could be clothes, toys, or even food. You could also donate your time by volunteering at a charity or participating in community activities.

Charities are organizations that are set up to help and support different causes. They support diverse groups of people, animals, and communities, and rely on donations of money or items to do their work and help their causes. There are many charities that focus on many different areas. Some focus on local causes, such as building and maintaining playgrounds, while others focus on global initiatives, such as providing relief after international disasters like floods or earthquakes.

When you make a donation to a charity, whether you give money or items, you are helping the charity to make a difference. Your contribution might be used to help children displaced by wars, protect animals in the wild, or find a cure for diseases.

Here are some examples of charities and the vital work they do:

- **UNICEF:** UNICEF promotes the well-being and health of children around the world. They work to ensure children have access to clean water, sanitation, education, and health care.
- **Habitat for Humanity:** Habitat for Humanity brings people together to build homes for those in need.

- **United Way:** United Way supports programs that aim to improve communities' education, health, and financial stability.
- **SPCA:** The SPCA (Society for the Prevention of Cruelty to Animals) supports animal care and safety. Their work aims to protect animals by providing rescue services and vets and educating the public about pet ownership.
- **Wounded Warrior Project:** The Wounded Warrior Project supports service members and veterans wounded while serving in the military.
- **Special Olympics:** The Special Olympics supports athletes with disabilities.
- **American Red Cross:** The American Red Cross supports crisis intervention and disaster relief locally and worldwide. Their work includes blood donations, medical training, and supplies during emergencies or disasters.

When people donate to these charities, they help to support their activities or causes. These charities' donations help people, animals, and the community. The more donations they receive, the more significant impact they can have on the lives of others and the community.

DID YOU KNOW? *UNICEF helps children in over 190 countries. Through their programs, they provide lifesaving vaccines to around 45% of the world's children and help ensure that millions have access to education, clean water, and emergency assistance.*

HOW TO FIND CHARITIES OR CAUSES YOU'RE PASSIONATE ABOUT

Finding a charity that you're passionate about can be an exciting journey.

Here are some steps to help you get started:

❶ Think about your interests.

The first thing you should do is think about what you're interested in. What do you enjoy doing? Who do you enjoy spending time with? The charity's work will mean much more if you can relate to it.

❷ Research charities online.

After you have thought about your interests, go online and do a search on "charities." You should come up with a list of relevant charities. Read about all the different ones to see if any do work related to your interests.

❸ Talk with an adult.

Talk with a parent or a trusted adult to see what knowledge or information they can share with you about their experience with charities.

❹ Volunteer at a local charity.

Find out which charities are local. Have an adult take you to visit some of these charities so you can experience them first-hand. While there, find out if you can volunteer at the charities that interest you.

❺ **Follow your passions.**

After gathering all the information you can about the various charities, revisit your interests and think about which ones you're passionate about. Then find the charity that is the closest match.

Remember, even a small act of kindness can have a big impact. By choosing to support a charity, you're not just giving money or time—you're helping to make the world a better place. Now, that's something to feel good about!

FINDING YOUR CHARITY

Making a difference in the world can be as simple as supporting a cause you believe in. Let's take a journey to find a charity that you really believe in.

1 **What matters to you:** What causes are you passionate about? Animals? Helping people in need? The environment? Write down a few causes that are important to you:

____

____

2 **Research charities:** Look up charities that work towards the causes that are important to you. Write them here:

____

____

3 **Evaluate the charities:** Look at how these charities use their money. Do they spend most of it on the cause they support, or do they spend it on other costs? Write down your findings:

____

____

4 **Pick your charity:** Based on your research, pick one charity you want to support:

____

5 **Plan your support:** Think about how you could support this charity. Could you donate some of your allowance? Or volunteer your time? Write down your plan here:

____

____

6 **Take action:** Once you have a plan, it's time to put it into action!

CHAPTER 6:

HOW TO KEEP YOUR MONEY SAFE AND SECURE

You put a lot of effort into earning your money, so it's crucial that you keep it safe. This includes the money in your bank account, the cash you carry, and any cards you use to withdraw money.

HOW TO PROTECT YOUR MONEY AND PERSONAL INFORMATION

Here are some tips to protect your money and personal information:

1. **Keep your money in a bank account:** Putting it in a bank account is a smart way to keep it safe and organized. When you open an account, remember to keep your personal information private and only share it with people or organizations you trust.

2. **Carry less cash:** Carrying a lot of money can make you more likely to lose it or have it stolen. Try to only carry the cash you need for the day to keep your money safe.

3. **Stay safe when spending money online:** Be super careful when buying things online to protect your financial information. Look for secure websites with "https" at the beginning of the web address. Only share personal data like your name, address, or social security number if you trust the website.
4. **Avoid saving card details on shared computers:** If you use a computer other people also use, don't save your credit or debit card details. Other people might be able to access your personal information, which could be risky.
5. **Create strong passwords:** When you create passwords for your online accounts, make them strong and unique. A strong password has a mix of numbers, lowercase and uppercase letters, and symbols. Remember not to use the same password for different accounts, and to change your passwords regularly to keep them extra secure.
6. **Don't share personal information online:** It's essential to keep your personal information private online. Avoid posting pictures of documents like your passport or bank statements with personal information. Keep your name, date of birth, address, and unique ID number to yourself to protect your identity.
7. **Keep your PINs private:** Your PINs are like secret codes, so never share them with anyone. Also, ensure no one can see you when you enter your PIN while making transactions. It's essential to keep your PINs safe and private.

By following these safety tips, you can keep your money and personal information secure. Remember, being cautious and protecting yourself from potential risks is always better.

DID YOU KNOW? *The most popular password is "123456." Using simple and predictable passwords like this can make it easy for hackers to access your accounts and steal your personal information. Choosing strong and unique passwords is vital for keeping your online accounts secure.*

WHAT ARE SCAMS?

Always keep your eyes and ears open for scams. Scams are deceptive schemes designed to cheat people out of their money, and they usually sound too good to be true.

Scammers will pretend to be someone else or from a well-known company to gain your trust. They may contact you through email, text, or phone, offering you what seems like a fantastic deal. They might ask you to click on a link in an email or text, or request personal information over the phone to gain access to your bank accounts or credit cards. That's why it's super important to never give out your personal information to anyone.

Scammers are clever, and they use many different strategies to trick people into giving away their personal information so they can get their money. Here are a few examples you should watch out for:

1. **Phishing scams:** These scams involve fake emails or messages that look like they're from a genuine company or person you know. They might ask you to click a link or log into an account. Be careful! The link usually takes you to a fake website that wants to steal your personal information. They might even send you an

email attachment that can harm your computer. Never click on links in suspicious emails or texts.

2. **Lottery and prize scams:** In these scams, scammers pretend that you've won a lottery, vacation, or prize. They might send you a letter or email, or call to congratulate you. But here's the catch: They'll ask you to pay fees up front or give them personal information to claim your prize. Be cautious and remember that real lotteries or prizes don't ask for money or personal information to receive your winnings.

3. **Online financial account scams:** Scammers might send you text messages or emails that seem to be from a bank or financial institution. They might claim there is a problem with your account and ask you to verify your information on a fake website. Remember, real banks will never ask you to provide personal details via email or text. If you receive such messages, don't click on any links. Instead, contact your bank directly.

4. **Card skimming:** This sneaky scam happens when scammers copy information from the magnetic strip of your debit, credit, or ATM card. They'll try to capture your PIN, bank, and credit card details to make unauthorized purchases. Be careful when using ATMs or card readers, and cover your hand while entering your PIN.

5. **Online shopping scams:** Beware of online sellers who promise great deals but deliver something that doesn't meet your expectations (or even nothing at all!). Some scammers use online shopping to collect your bank account or credit card information. Make sure to buy from trusted websites and read reviews from other customers before purchasing.

6. **Charity scams:** Unfortunately, even charity causes can be used by scammers. They might pretend to work for an actual charity and try to collect money from you. They often use recent crises or natural disasters to play with your emotions. If you want to donate, research the charity first and donate directly through their official website.

> ***DID YOU KNOW?*** *Scams and money fraud cost the global economy over $5 trillion annually. That's more money than the entire economy of a big country like the United Kingdom!*

HOW TO RECOGNIZE SCAMS AND FRAUD

While scams may not be easy to spot, there are some things to look for that may indicate a possible fraud:

- They ask for money upfront.
- You receive offers that you didn't ask for.
- You receive a message from a number you don't recognize, asking you to click on a link.
- You receive a phone call, email, or text from someone claiming to be from an official department, like the government, fire department, or your bank, asking for money.
- You feel pressured to make a quick decision.
- They request that money be wired, sent by a courier, or transferred through a gift or prepaid card.

- They request access to your bank accounts, credit cards, or ATM cards.
- They offer you a deal that sounds too good to be true, but avoid answering any questions you may have.

If you come across any of these signs or feel unsure about a situation, talk to your parents or a trusted adult.

WHAT TO DO IF YOU SPOT A SCAM

If you come across something that seems like a scam, it's essential to take action to protect yourself. Here's what you should do:

1. **Trust your instincts:** If something doesn't feel right or seems too good to be true, it's better to be cautious.
2. **Stop communicating and don't share any information:** Stop communicating with them and don't provide them with any personal information.
3. **Tell your parents:** If something doesn't feel right, talk to your parents or a trusted adult. It's better to be safe than sorry.
4. **Report the scam:** You can report scams online or via phone to the Federal Trade Commission (FTC). They are a government agency that investigates scams and protects people from fraud.

Unfortunately, scams are a regular part of everyday life. Still, by understanding how to spot them and being cautious, you can help to protect yourself.

Creating a strong password is one of the best ways to protect yourself and your financial information online. Here's a simple activity to help you create strong passwords that are easy for you to remember, but difficult for fraudsters to guess.

ACTIVITY TIME!

CREATING A STRONG PASSWORD

1 **Start with a base word or phrase**

Choose a word or phrase that is easy for you to remember. It could be something related to your interests or a favorite hobby.

For example, let's use the base word "guitar."

2 **Mix in numbers**

Add a series of numbers to your base word. You can choose numbers that are meaningful to you, such as your birthdate or a special number.

For our example, let's use the number "2023."

3 **Incorporate special characters**

Include special characters, like exclamation marks, question marks, or hashtags, to add complexity to your password. Pick a special character that you can easily remember.

For our example, we'll use the exclamation mark!

4 **Use capitalization**

Change the capitalization of some letters in your base word to make it even stronger. Mix uppercase and lowercase letters to make it harder to guess.

In our example, let's capitalize the letter "G" in "Guitar."

5 **Combine and personalize**

Put all the elements together to create your strong password. In our example, the final password would be "Guitar2023!" Remember, don't use this example as your password. Instead, create your unique combination based on your interests and the steps provided.

Now it's your turn

CREATING A STRONG PASSWORD

OVER TO YOU

1. Choose a base word or phrase:

____

2. Add a series of numbers:

____

3. Incorporate a special character:

____

4. Change the capitalization of some letters:

____

5. Combine all the elements to create your strong password:

____

Congratulations!

You've created a strong password by following these steps.

REMEMBER

- Always keep your password secure.
- Don't share it with anyone.
- Avoid using easily guessable information like your name, address, or common words.
- Use different passwords for different accounts to maximize security.

CHAPTER 7:

AN INTRODUCTION TO INVESTING

You've learned the importance of earning money, saving it, and spending it wisely. But what if there was a way to make your money work for you, even while you're not using it? Instead of simply setting your money aside, what if you could make it grow! Welcome to the world of investing. Let's explore how this process works and how it can help you achieve your financial goals!

WHAT IS INVESTING?

Imagine you have some money you earned from doing chores, or that you received as a gift. You can keep that money safe by putting it in a piggy bank, or earn interest by depositing it in a savings account. When you save money, you're setting it aside for a specific purpose at a later date, like buying a toy or saving up for something special. It's like keeping your money safe for later.

But what if you could make that money do more than just sit and wait for you? What if your money could work for you and even multiply? That's where investing comes in!

Investing is a way to use your money to make even more money over time. Instead of just keeping it in a piggy bank, you can grow your money by putting it into things that might increase in value. It's like planting a seed and watching it grow into a big tree.

> *For example, let's say you love playing video games and notice that a certain company that makes video games, like Nintendo or Sony, is doing well. You can buy a small part of that company by purchasing some of its stocks. Stocks are like tiny pieces of the company that you can own. When the company does well, the value of your stocks might go up, and you can sell them later at a higher price. This is how you can make money by investing!*
>
> *But if the company doesn't do so well and the stock value goes down, the value of your stocks may decrease. This means you could lose money if you decide to sell your shares at a lower price.*

The main difference between saving and investing is the growth potential. When you save money, it usually stays the same or earns a small amount of interest. But when you invest, you take a calculated risk in the hopes that your money will grow even more.

Saving  Investing

SAVING

Putting money aside to use at a later date

INVESTING

Putting money into something to make it grow over time

Saving is good for short-term goals, like buying a new toy or saving for a special occasion. On the other hand, investing is usually for long-term goals, like saving for college or retirement. It's about using your money to potentially make more money over a longer period of time.

It's important to understand that investing always comes with some level of risk. The value of stocks can go up and down, and sometimes you may even lose money. It requires careful consideration and research, and is a long-term commitment. If you're interested in investing, it's a good idea to learn more and seek guidance from trusted adults or professionals who can help you make informed decisions.

Ways to Invest

Stocks

Stocks are small parts of a company. If the company does well, your part may grow. If they do badly, your part may be worth less.

Bonds

When you buy a bond, you are lending your money to a company or the government. Usually with a fixed interest rate.

Real Estate

Real estate involves investing in property. You make money by renting or selling the property for a profit.

Mutual Funds

Mutual funds include a bunch of different stocks, or other things like bonds or real estate, all in one package.

Exchange Traded Funds (ETFs)

An ETF is like a basket that holds a collection of different investments designed to track or follow the performance of a specific market index, like the S&P 500.

DIFFERENT WAYS TO INVEST MONEY

There are lots of different ways to invest money. Here are some of the most common:

- **Stocks:** When you invest in stocks, you buy a tiny share of a company. If the company does well, the stock may go up. If you sell your stocks at a higher price than what you paid for them, you make money.

  For example, let's say you buy a share of a company called ABC Toys for $10. You now own a small part of the company. If ABC Toys does well, the stock might go up. Let's say that, after a year, the stock is now worth $15 per share, and you decide to sell your share at a higher price. In that case, you'd make a profit of $5 ($15–$10).

- **Bonds:** Bonds are like loans. When you buy a bond, you are lending your money to a company or the government. They promise to pay you back the money you lent them, plus interest. Bonds are considered less risky than stocks, so the money you make from them is usually lower.
- **Real Estate:** Real estate involves investing in properties, like houses or apartments. When you invest in real estate, you can make money in two ways. First, by renting the property. Second, by selling the property for more money than you originally paid.
- **Mutual Funds:** Mutual funds are like a team of investments. Instead of buying just one stock, you can buy a fund that includes a bunch of different stocks, or other things like bonds or real estate, all in one package. This can help reduce your risk, because if one investment doesn't do well, others may do better and balance it out.

- **Exchange Traded Funds (ETFs):** Just like a mutual fund, an ETF is like a basket that holds a collection of different investments designed to track or follow the performance of a specific market index, like the S&P 500. ETFs are popular because they spread your money and reduce risk.

> ***DID YOU KNOW?*** *The most valuable company in the world in 2023 is Apple. With a market value of almost $3 trillion, Apple has become a technology giant known for its innovative products like iPhones, iPads, and Mac computers.*

UNDERSTANDING RISK AND RETURNS

Risk involves the possibility of losing money. When you invest, there's a chance you might not get back all the money you put in.

Return, on the other hand, is the amount of money your investment can make. Some investments have the potential for higher returns, while others offer lower returns.

> *Imagine you've got $10. You have a choice: You could spend it on a cool toy car, which you know will keep some value over time. You can play with the car, and, when you're done, perhaps you can sell it to a friend for a little less than what you paid for. This is a type of low-risk investment. You're pretty sure you won't lose all your money, and you might even make a little bit of money if you find the right buyer.*
>
> *Now picture this: Instead of getting that toy car, you buy a trading card for the same $10. It's not just any card—it's a card that could become*

rare and valuable over time. There's a chance that other collectors might be willing to pay a lot more for it in a year or two. But if the card doesn't become as popular as you thought, you might not be able to sell it for what you paid. This is a riskier investment. The possibility of making more money is there, but so is the possibility of losing some.

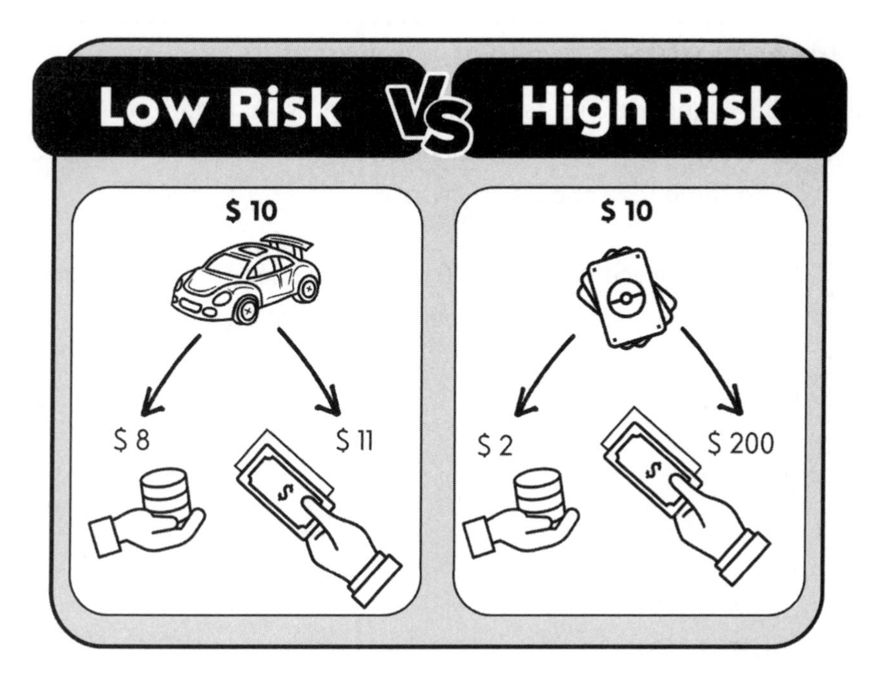

That's the essence of investing—using your money to make more money, but with the understanding that there are different levels of risk involved.

When you invest, you have to think about how much risk you're willing to take. If you take more risk, there's a chance for a higher return, which means you could make more money. If you take less risk, the potential return might not be as much, but you're also less likely to lose money.

Investing is like a game where you must make smart choices and consider possible risks and rewards. It's essential to do your research, ask for advice from grown-ups you trust, and remember that investing is a long-term plan.

UNDERSTANDING COMPOUND GROWTH

Remember when we discussed compound interest, where your money earns interest on the initial amount and the interest you've already made? The same idea applies to investing.

Let's imagine you start with $10 and your money doubles every day for 10 days. How much money would you have at the end?

Day 1: $10
Day 2: $20
Day 3: $40
Day 4: $80
Day 5: $160
Day 6: $320
Day 7: $640
Day 8: $1,280
Day 9: $2,560
Day 10: $5,120

As you can see, the amount of money you have is getting bigger and bigger each day. But something interesting happens as you go along. In the beginning, the growth might not seem very big.

For example, from $10 to $20 is a $10 increase. But, as you get closer to the end, the growth becomes much larger. Going from $2,560 to $5,120 is a $2,560 increase!

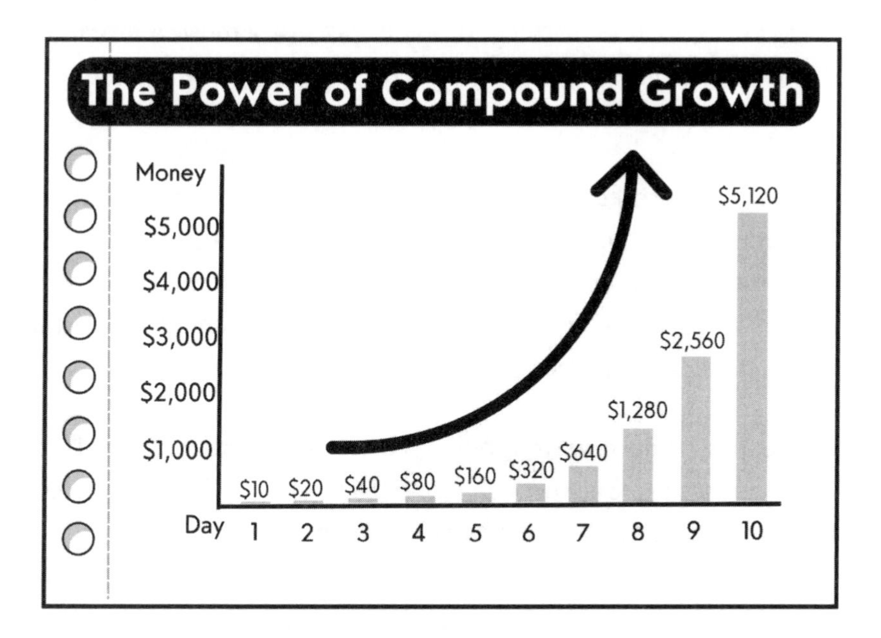

That's because compound growth makes your money grow faster over time. It's like a snowball rolling down a hill, getting bigger and faster as it goes. The more time your money stays invested, the more it can grow.

When you invest, it's essential to be patient and let your money work for you. Sometimes, the value might go down, but, if you give it time, it's likely to bounce back and grow even more.

Starting early is vital. The longer you leave your money invested, the more it can grow. Starting early gives you a better chance of achieving financial success and seeing your money grow bigger and bigger.

UNLOCKING THE POWER OF COMPOUND GROWTH IN EVERYDAY LIFE

This concept of compound growth applies not only to money, but to anything in life, such as learning to play a sport or a musical instrument. It's the idea that minor improvements or progress made over time can lead to significant results.

> *Imagine you're learning to play the guitar. If you practice for just a few minutes every day, you'll gradually get better. But, if you practice consistently for longer periods, over months and years, you'll become even more skilled. The more you practice, the more you'll learn and the better you'll become.*

Like investing, where your money grows over time, your skills and abilities can also grow through consistent effort. The key is to be patient, keep practicing, and stay committed to your goals.

THE IMPORTANCE OF DIVERSIFICATION AND LONG-TERM INVESTING

Diversification is a smart strategy for reducing the risk of your investments by spreading your money across different types of things you invest in. These things are called assets, and you buy them with the hope that they'll increase in value over time.

> *Let's use a trading card collection as an example.*
>
> *Instead of just buying baseball cards, you might also buy Pokemon or Yu-gi-oh cards. That way, if the value of baseball cards doesn't go up, there's still a chance that the Pokemon or Yu-gi-oh cards will increase*

in value. Having different types of cards in your collection increases the chances of making money, even if one type doesn't do well.

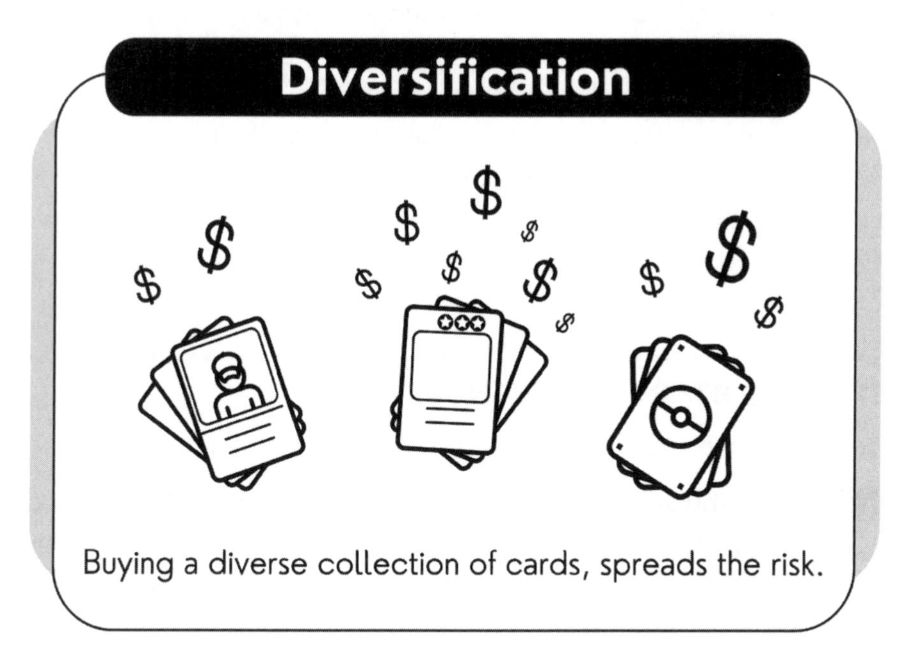

Buying a diverse collection of cards, spreads the risk.

Investing in a mix of assets means that even if some of your investments don't do so well, others might do better. It's like having a balance. Overall, diversification reduces the risk of losing money and gives you a better chance of earning more in the long run. It's a way to protect your investments and increase the possibility of making more money.

HOW CAN TEENS INVEST THEIR MONEY?

Investing can be exciting. While you may not be able to open your own investment account if you're under 18, you can still get started by partnering with an adult, like a parent or guardian, to open a custodial account.

A custodial account is a particular type of investment account where the adult manages the investments on your behalf until you reach the legal age to handle the account on your own. It's a great way to learn about investing and start growing your money, even at a young age.

Even though you may not be able to have your own investment account yet, you can still take advantage of the opportunity to invest and build wealth for your future. It's never too early to start learning about money and making smart financial decisions.

STEPS TO START INVESTING

Here are some steps to help you get started with investing:

1. **Learn about investing:** Take the time to read and learn about investing. You can find books, articles, and videos that explain the basics. Talk to an adult with investing experience and ask them to share their knowledge.

2. **Set your goals:** Consider what you want to achieve with your investments. Do you want to save for college, buy a car, or have money for the future? Setting clear goals will help you make investment decisions that align with your objectives.

3. **Choose your investments:** Research different investment options, such as stocks or mutual funds. Look for companies or funds you are interested in and that you believe have growth potential. Remember to consider the level of risk and potential returns.

4. **Open a custodial account:** Since you are under 18, you will need an adult to help you open a custodial account. This special

type of account allows an adult to manage the investments on your behalf until you are old enough to handle it yourself.

5. **Invest your money:** Once you have chosen your investments, you can start putting your money into them. Use a trusted investment platform, like a bank or brokerage firm, to make your purchases. Always consult the adult managing your custodial account to ensure you use a legitimate platform.

6. **Start small and be cautious:** It's a good idea to start with a small amount of money that you can afford to invest. As you gain more experience and confidence, you can consider investing larger amounts. Remember, investing involves risks, so it's important to be cautious and only invest money you are potentially willing to lose.

By following these steps and seeking guidance from trusted adults, you can begin your investing journey and work towards achieving your financial goals.

ACTIVITY: DOUBLE THE PENNY CHALLENGE

Let's have some fun with the "Double Penny Challenge" to see just how powerful compound interest can be!

This simple challenge will help illustrate the concept of compound interest, when you earn interest on both the money you've saved and the interest you earned.

Once you've finished the exercise reflect: How does seeing this growth make you feel about saving money? Do you think it's a good idea to start saving as soon as possible?

Remember, this challenge is just an illustration of how compound interest can help grow your savings. In real life, money won't double daily, but over time, with regular savings and the power of compound interest, you can see your money grow in a similar way.

The lesson is: start saving early and save regularly! Even if it seems like a small amount, over time, it can grow into a substantial sum.

DOUBLE THE PENNY CHALLENGE

INSTRUCTIONS

Make Your Choice

Would you rather have a penny that doubles each day for a month or $1 million?

- ☐ A Penny that Doubles Every Day
- ☐ $1 million

- Write down your amounts for each day on the line provided inside the piggy banks. (You may need a calculator!)
- Start with a penny on the first day.
- On the following day, double the amount.
- Keep doubling the amount until you reach the 30th day.

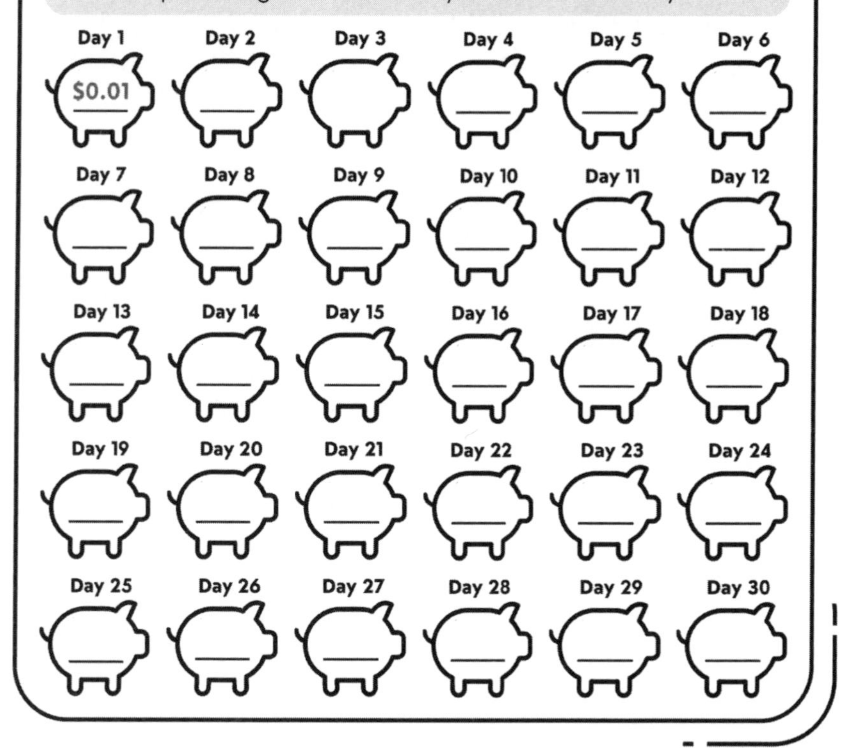

CHAPTER 8:

PLANNING FOR THE FUTURE

You've come a long way on your financial journey! From earning money to investing it wisely, you're already on the path to a bright financial future. But did you know that there's more you can do to ensure your future is even brighter?

Let's take a look at planning for the future and taking responsibility for your finances.

TAKING RESPONSIBILITY FOR YOUR FINANCES

Planning for your future is a crucial part of being financially successful. It's never too early to start planning. The sooner you begin, the better off you'll be.

As you grow older, you'll take on more financial responsibilities, like pursuing a career, buying a house, and getting a car. But there are other costs involved that you might not be aware of.

Let's take a look at some of these future financial responsibilities:

Future Financial Responsibilities

Taxes 	Fees paid to fund public services and programs like schools and emergency services. The amount you pay is generally based on a percentage of your income.
Insurance 	Protects you from paying a lot of money if something unexpected happens. There are different types of insurance, such as health insurance and insurance for your belongings.
Retirement 	When you stop working and need money to support yourself. Before that time comes, you need to set aside or invest some money.

Taxes

Taxes are fees paid to the government to fund public services and programs like schools and emergency services. If you earn money, you'll likely have to pay taxes of some kind. The amount you pay is generally based on a percentage of your income. The higher your salary, the higher the rate of tax you have to pay.

> *For example, if you earn $25,000, you may only pay 10% tax, or $2,500. However, if you earn $100,000, you may pay a higher percentage (such as 37%) in taxes, which would amount to $37,000.*

If you work for a company, your employer will automatically take out a portion of your earnings to pay your taxes. They do this to make sure your taxes are paid throughout the year. This system is called tax withholding.

But if you're self-employed, like a freelancer or independent contractor, you are responsible for calculating and paying your taxes. This means you must figure out how much tax you owe and pay it yourself.

Insurance

Insurance is like a safety net that helps protect you from financial loss. It's important to know that insurance works differently in different countries. Not all countries have the same types of insurance, or even require you to have it.

> *For example, in some countries, like the United States, there is health insurance. Health insurance helps cover the cost of medical expenses, like going to the doctor or getting medicine.*
>
> *If you have health insurance, you pay a monthly or yearly amount called a premium to an insurance company. In return, the insurance company helps pay some of your medical costs when needed. Some companies may offer health insurance as part of their employee benefits.*

Another type of insurance is for your belongings, like your house or car. If something terrible happens, like a fire in your home or an accident with your vehicle, insurance can help cover the cost of repairing or replacing them. You pay a premium to the insurance company, and if something happens, they pay for losses or damages.

Having insurance is like having a backup plan. It helps protect you from paying a lot of money if something unexpected happens. Just like you wear a helmet while riding a bike to protect your head, insurance is there to protect your finances.

Retirement

Finally, there's planning for retirement. Retirement is when you stop working and need money to support yourself. It may seem like a long way off right now, but it's helpful to start thinking about it early in order to have a comfortable life when you're older.

Preparing for retirement means saving money for the future. The idea is to set aside and invest a portion of your income once you start earning so you have enough money to live on later when you're no longer working.

In most countries, there are specific retirement accounts, like a 401(k) or an individual retirement account (IRA) in the United States, that have rules and benefits to help your money grow.

Remember, the key is to start saving and investing for your retirement early. The more time your money has to grow and compound, the more you'll have when you retire.

DID YOU KNOW? *That the average retirement age in the United States has been gradually increasing over the years. As of 2021, the average age for retirement was around 66 years old.*

PREPARING FOR YOUR FUTURE

It's never too early to start thinking about your future and how you want to live. Even before you finish school, you can begin to explore what excites you and what you're passionate about.

Finding the right job isn't just about making money. It's about finding something you enjoy and are good at. Explore your hobbies and skills, and ask yourself: What are you good at? What do you love to do? Learn about different careers and the education or training required, so you can make smart decisions for your future.

When you think about your future, it's essential to consider what makes you happy and excited. Talk to people in various professions and explore different options. Maybe you're interested in helping animals, creating artwork, or building things. No matter what your passion is, there are many paths you can take to turn it into a fulfilling career.

Your future is full of possibilities, and you have the power to shape it into something incredible. The choices you make now, like studying hard and exploring your interests, can help you create a life that reflects your passions and dreams. Remember, finding a job you love means you'll enjoy your work, and it won't feel like just a job. Your future is in your hands, so dream big and follow your passions!

THINKING ABOUT FUTURE EXPENSES: PLANNING AND SAVING

As you grow older, you'll have bigger dreams and plans. Maybe you'll want to go to college, start a business, or travel the world. It's a good idea to start thinking about these goals early and figure out how you can save up for them.

By setting aside a little bit of money regularly, you can build up your savings over time. This way, when the time comes to pay for your big plans, you'll have some money saved up to help you get started.

Remember, it's not just about having enough money for these goals. It's also about learning to plan ahead and being responsible with your finances. And the best part is, even if you're saving a small amount, it can add up over time and make a big difference.

So, start thinking about what you might want to do in the future and how you can save up for it. Every bit of planning and saving helps you get closer to achieving your dreams.

THE IMPORTANCE OF FINANCIAL INDEPENDENCE

As you grow older, you'll look forward to the time when you can move out of your parent's home and live on your own. This is when you'll need to support yourself using your own money to pay for everything you need. It's called financial independence.

Reaching the stage of financial independence is something to be proud of. It feels great to know that, when the time is right, you can take care of yourself without relying on others for financial help.

Here are the steps that lead to financial independence.

1. **Earning money:** Find a job and work hard to start making money. The earlier you start, the sooner you can work toward financial independence.
2. **Saving money:** Put a portion of your earnings into savings so that your money can grow over time through earned interest. This will also ensure you have money available for future expenses.

3. **Spending money wisely:** Use your money wisely, avoiding unnecessary expenses. Creating a budget will help you differentiate between what you need and what you want, keeping you on track toward financial independence.
4. **Investing money:** Once you have an emergency fund set aside and some extra money each month, you can think about investing. Investing is another way to potentially make your money grow over time.
5. **Planning for the future:** It's a good idea to start planning for future expenses before you become financially independent. By doing so, you'll have a head-start and already have some money set aside for those future needs.

Steps to Financial Independence

Earning money	Find a job and work hard to start making money.
Saving Money	Save money, earn interest and have money available for future expenses.
Spend Money Wisely	Avoid unnecessary expenses. Creating a budget will be a big help on this.
Invest Money	Potentially make your money grow over time.
Planning for the future	Plan ahead towards future expenses and set aside money for it.

Congratulations! You've reached financial independence! You've taken the necessary steps to earn, save, spend wisely, and plan for the future. Now, you have the confidence and freedom to care for yourself and live the life you've always dreamed of. Well done!

DISCOVER YOUR PERFECT CAREER

This activity is all about exploring your interests, passions, and aspirations. There are no right or wrong answers. Use your imagination and dream big about the possibilities for your future career!

1. Think about the things you enjoy doing and the subjects you find interesting.

   a) What are your favorite subjects in school?

   ____

   b) What topics or subjects do you enjoy learning about outside of school?

   ____

   c) What are your favorite hobbies or activities?

   ____

   d) Is there a cause or issue that you feel passionate about?

   ____

2. Look at your answers and consider how they relate to different career options. Write down any careers that come to mind based on your interests and passions.

   ____________ ____________

   ____________ ____________

   ____________ ____________

3. Now, consider what you want to achieve or contribute through your career.

   a) What are your favorite subjects in school?

   ____

   b) How would you like to help others or make a difference?

   ____

   c) What skills or talents do you have that could be valuable in a career?

   ____

4. Look at your answers and reflect on the careers that align with your interests, passions, and goals. Write down any additional jobs that you discover based on this reflection.

_______________ _______________

_______________ _______________

_______________ _______________

5. Take a moment to review your answers and consider the connections or patterns you notice. Write down any observations or thoughts about your ideal career path.

____

____

6. **Share and discuss:** If you feel comfortable, share your answers with a friend, family member, or teacher. Discuss your interests, passions, and the careers you discovered. Listen to their thoughts and feedback.

6. **Dream Big:** Imagine yourself in your perfect career. What does it look like? How does it make you feel? Write or draw your vision here.

CONCLUSION

Congratulations on starting your journey to learn about money skills! By understanding and applying the concepts we discussed, you are taking the first steps toward financial success. Remember, this is just the beginning of your lifelong journey of managing money responsibly.

When it comes to money, success means knowing how to take care of it from the very start. This begins from the moment you start earning an allowance, goes on to when you have your first part-time job, and continues throughout your entire life.

Once you start earning money, don't forget the power of saving. Consider opening a savings account where a portion of your earnings can stay safe and grow over time. Just like a tree needs time to grow from a seed, your savings also need time to grow.

Spending money wisely is another critical part of handling money responsibly. It's about making thoughtful decisions when you're about to buy something. Every time you spend money, ask yourself if you're spending it on something you need or just something you want. Make sure your needs are met that and you've put some of your money in savings before you spend money on things you just want. Before buying anything, do some detective work. Compare prices, read reviews, and consider the long-term costs and benefits.

When you buy something online or in a store, you may use a debit or credit card, or maybe even the "Buy Now Pay Later" option. Be aware that if you use a credit card or "Buy Now Pay Later," you could be charged interest, which means you may end up paying more for the item in the long run.

A smart way to keep track of your earnings and spending is by setting up a budget and sticking to it. Think of your budget like a roadmap for your money, helping you avoid the bumpy road of debt, meet your savings goals, and feel confident about managing your money.

Remember, money isn't just about earning, saving, and spending. It's also about giving. Whether it's your time, money, things, or just a kind word or smile, sharing with others can make a big difference and make someone's day a little brighter.

You'll also want to keep your money safe. This means not sharing your personal details, only shopping on secure websites, not carrying lots of cash, and always keeping an eye out for tricks or scams.

While keeping your money safe is crucial, you'll want it to grow, too. This is where investing comes into play. Do your research, start small, and always think long term. Investing isn't about getting rich quickly, it's about gradually building wealth over time.

Taking care of your money responsibly is key to being stable financially, making smart decisions, and reaching your long-term financial goals. It means developing a budget, saving regularly, investing wisely, spending smartly to avoid debt, and working towards being financially independent so that you can enjoy a secure financial future.

Remember, the journey doesn't end here. Continuously learning about handling money effectively will help you make smarter financial choices throughout your life. There are always new things to discover and ways to improve your money skills.

Keep exploring, keep learning, and keep growing. Your financial future is in your hands, and with the knowledge and skills you've gained, you have the power to shape it and achieve your dreams. Embrace the journey, and may it lead you to a lifetime of financial success!

Good luck!

GLOSSARY OF KEY FINANCIAL TERMS

1. **Cash:** Cash is what you probably think of when you hear the word "money." It's the paper bills and metal coins that you can use to buy things. You can also save it or even invest it to help it grow!

2. **Income:** Income is the money that you earn. This could come from doing chores, working at a part-time job, or even making a video that people pay to watch (like on YouTube).

3. **Expenses:** Expenses are what you spend your money on. This could be anything from a new video game to a meal at a restaurant, or even paying for a bus ride. Sometimes, you have to plan ahead for big expenses in the future, like saving for a bike or even thinking about college.

4. **Needs vs. wants:** "Needs" are things you must have to survive, like food and shelter. "Wants" are things that are nice to have, but that you don't absolutely need, like toys or video games. Knowing the difference can help you make good spending decisions.

5. **Budget:** A budget is like a map for your money. It helps you keep track of how much money you're earning (your income), how much you're spending (your expenses), and how much you're

saving. It's a tool to help you manage your money and reach your goals.

6. **Saving:** Saving is when you put some of your money aside for later. It's like planting a seed that can grow over time. The sooner you start to save, the bigger your money "tree" can grow. This is thanks to something called interest, which can make your savings grow even when you're not adding more to it.

7. **Interest:** Interest can work in two ways. It's the money you earn from saving or investing over time, but it is also the extra money you pay when you borrow money. It's like a reward for saving and a cost for borrowing.

8. **Compound interest:** Compound interest is when your interest starts earning its own interest! It's like a snowball rolling down a hill, getting bigger and bigger. It's a powerful way to help your savings or investments grow over time.

9. **Investing:** Investing is a way to make your money work for you. It's like giving your money a job! For example, you could buy a small part of a company (that's called buying stocks), and if the company does well, your money could grow. Spreading your money into different types of investments is called diversification, and it can help protect your money from ups and downs in the market.

10. **Debt:** Debt is money you've borrowed and need to repay. This could be money you borrowed from a friend to buy lunch when you forgot your wallet, or it could be a significant amount, like a loan to buy a house when you're older. It's important to pay back debt quickly because the longer it takes to pay it back, the more it can cost you in fees or interest.

11. **Credit card:** A credit card is a plastic card issued by a bank or a financial institution. It allows you to buy things now and pay for them later. However, if you don't pay back the money by a specific date, you could be charged extra money called "interest."

12. **Debit card:** A debit card is another plastic card linked directly to your bank account. When you buy something with a debit card, the money is immediately taken out of your account. It's like digital cash!

13. **Taxes:** Taxes are payments that people make to the government. They help pay for things like schools, roads, and public services. You might not have to worry about these yet, but it's good to know about them for the future!

14. **Financial independence:** Financial independence is when you have enough money to take care of yourself without needing help from others. It's a big goal for when you're older, and being good with money now can help you reach it. Being financially responsible is a big part of this, and it starts with understanding these concepts!

THANKS
FOR READING OUR
BOOK!

I hope it has been helpful in teaching your kids important money skills that will serve them well throughout their life.

I would be so grateful if you could take a few seconds to leave an honest review or a star rating on Amazon. (A star rating takes just a couple of clicks).

By leaving a review, you'll be helping other parents discover this money skills book for their kids. Thank you!

Scan the code to leave a review & help spread the word: